POETRY NOW

SOUTH WEST 1996

Edited by Andrew Head

First published in Great Britain in 1996 by
POETRY NOW
1-2 Wainman Road, Woodston,
Peterborough, PE2 7BU

All Rights Reserved

Copyright Contributors 1995

SB ISBN 1 85731 667 3

FOREWORD

Although we are a nation of poetry writers we are accused of not reading poetry and not buying poetry books: after many years of listening to the incessant gripes of poetry publishers, I can only assume that the books they publish, in general, are books that most people do not want to read.

Poetry should not be obscure, introverted, and as cryptic as a crossword puzzle: it is the poet's duty to reach out and embrace the world.

The world owes the poet nothing and we should not be expected to dig and delve into a rambling discourse searching for some inner meaning.

The reason we write poetry (and almost all of us do) is because we want to communicate: an ideal; an idea; or a specific feeling. Poetry is as essential in communication, as a letter; a radio; a telephone, and the main criteria for selecting the poems in this anthology is very simple: they communicate.

Faced with hundreds of poems and a limited amount of space, the task of choosing the final poems was difficult and as editor one tries to be as detached as possible (quite often editors can become a barrier in the writer-reader exchange) acting as go between, making the connection, not censoring because of personal taste.

In this anthology over two hundred and ten poems are presented to the reader for their enjoyment.

The poetry is written on all levels; the simple and the complex both having their own appeal.

The success of this collection, and all previous *Poetry Now* anthologies, relies on the fact that there are as many individual readers as there are writers, and in the diversity of styles and forms there really is something to please, excite, and hopefully, inspire everyone who reads the book.

CONTENTS

The Family	Annette Furniss	1
Continuo	Peter Coxhead	2
Written In Belfast II	Ken Chalmers	2
Baby On The Beach	Wilma Jayne Gravenor	3
The Candle	Deane Stuart Wynne	3
Coast Walk	Charmian Astbury	4
Dark Nights	Linda Casey	4
Tower Of Strength	Marina Bell	5
Dreckly	Jeanne Short	6
The Sandpiper's Lament	Arnold Bloomer	7
For The Kingdom's Sake	Andrew Jones	8
An Ending	R M Lancaster	8
The Chill Of Silence	Kendall Lacey	9
Why Cry You Still?	Dean Smith	9
Rainbow	Nicola van Koutrik	10
Moor	Ben Morland	10
An Airfield At War	Matthew Turpin	11
Picture Box Crime	Matthew Barnes	11
Rain Rain Go Away	Constance Burniston	12
Drowning	G R Sowden	12
I Know A Magic Land	Hilary Greensmith	13
The Mourning	Anthony Lane	14
No Ships At French Weir	Nick Haines	15
In Loving Memory Of The Old Fiddler!	Naomi Wheelwright	16
Before Dawn On Cornish Moors	Diana Member	16
Porthmeor Beach	Alex Langstone	17
History Going	G James	17
Camelot	L Faulkner	18
The Key	T Tucker	19
Sunstarved	Susan Burgess	20
The Best In Life	Jeanette Harris	20
On The Occasion Of Our Son's Wedding	Paul Langford	21
Deflated At The Eisteddfod	W E Dinneen	22
Castle Beach	S Winfield	22

Yesterday	Lindsay Atfield	23
Drought 1995	M M R Greenaway	24
Untitled	Gerry Doe	24
Horn Of A Bull, Hoof Of A Horse, Smile Of A Saxon	Anna Forsyth	25
Elmer's Music	R Midwinter	26
The Garden	Marcella Pellow	26
Mirror Mirror On The Wall . . . Who . . .	N G Cooper	27
The Silence At Come-To-Good	Donald Rawe	28
The Course To End All Courses	Nora Mostyn-Bond	29
The Giro	Kathleen Schmidt	30
Autumn Mist In Roborough	Diana H Adams	30
Remembering	Irene Mooney	31
Out On The Marshes	J A Collinge	32
The Calling	Hannah Julian	32
The White Giants Of Garland Cross	Joan Hewitt	33
January	Martin Summers	34
Village In November	Ray Calaz	34
God's Love	A Roberts	35
Fairies	Leanne Taylor	36
Stones Thrown Away	G S Riggs	36
Blue Tears I Cry On Wednesday	Lee Robinson	37
My Sister Has Long Hair	Maureen Given	38
A Child's Memory	Pat W Hillyer	39
Winter	Natalie J Barker	40
Max	Lynda Callard	40
Schoolboy	P Powell	41
Beauty	Jill Allen	42
No Tears For Me	Mabel Mills	42
Mask	Frances Thompson	43
A Prison Boy	Sebina Clare Heffernan	44
Autumn Breeze	Anne H Brooks	44

The Stone	Victoria Pretty	45
Secret	Caroline Tiernan-Locke	45
Amelia's Cat	Jean Bitmead	46
Lady 'O'	P A Windsar	46
Golden Days	Lydia Stanton	47
Force 10 Imminent	David Dudley	48
Untitled	D A Russell	48
Sadly Missed By All	Emma Francis	49
Killing Angels	Thomas Paul Gidman	50
To A Shot Bird	Wendy Hooper	51
I Wasn't Born In Somerset	Patricia Catling	52
Biggy	Gwenda Jenkins	53
How?	Heather Nelson	54
Eating For Health	A Cotter	54
A Potential Hero	Kate Ellis	55
From The Heart	P C Gooding	56
Chelsea Flower Show	Paddy Jupp	56
Dreaming By The Shore	Val Callicott	57
Jewel Of Cornwall (St Michael's Mount, Marazion)	Elaine Pomm	57
Of Balloons And Bubbles	Winifred Rickard	58
Beeches In Autumn	Thomas Duggan	58
Forgotten Freedom	Karen Cook	59
Poppies	Ruby Charlton	60
Twilight	D A Hynes	60
Changing Times	Bernard Grose	61
Moon, Metal And Glance	J Guy	62
Crossroads	D J Smith	62
Drugs Poem	Kali Heffernan	63
The Yawning Bear	N J Steel	64
Feelings	Dee Kimber	64
Starters Boom	Eric Drake	65
Gifts Of Autumn	Carol Alway	65
The Embrace	Kate Tilley	66
Learned And Learner	Clifford J D Hart	66
Bosnia? Or Anywhere	S R Lucie	67
Peace	John Mostyn-Bond	67

Elective Mute	Rosie Cornish	68
Earth Mother	Teresa Webster	69
Never Worse Off	R Morris	70
Sunday	Rita Parfitt	71
Song Of A West Country Woman	Anne Pethereck	72
Lundy Folk	Jimmie Cross	73
The Gossamer Hour	Annabelle Ough	73
Mid-Week Break	Damon Naile	74
A Dartmoor Nonsense	Peter Lee	74
The Billiard Room Has Gone	Carol Exten-Wright	75
Grandma	R Ninnis	76
Thought	Chichieun Wong	76
The Passing Of Puss!	G Halfpenny	77
Granf	Margaret Whitehead	78
The Old Lady	Sally Wyatt	79
Torment	Andrew Carter	80
I Love You	V Stock	81
This Life Of Extremes	Norrie Hill	82
The Canals Of England	Alan Potter	83
The Seasons	J Hawkins	84
Inspiration	Laura David	84
Flowers Of The Field	Miranda Hodder	85
The Tiny Seed Of Love	Lucille Hope	86
Marine Drive	Leonard Fifield	87
Snow In Cornwall	Francis Middleditch	88
Caesar - The Cat	Anne Cleife	89
October	Diana Stannus	89
The Spirit Of Place	Grenville Gilbert	90
New Age	Chris Glover	90
Dartmoor, The Mystique	Edward A Walker	91
Springtime In Devon	Carol Diane Milne	92
The Spotted Fly Catcher	Phyl Williams	93
Untitled	Nur-Viktoria Frings	94
Powerhouses Of The Past	Roberta Gilman-Grey	94
Cornwall	Christine Willis	95
Plymouth - Resurgam	Alice Tall	96
Foster Mother	Roberta Bell	97

Bullying!	Lisa Tonkin	98
Six Swans; One Small Girl And A Camera	Richard Flemington	99
Old Age	V Murton	100
The Child That Never Was	Anne Harper	100
Ode To The Blackdowns	Brenda Eyles	101
The River	Paul Cox	102
Temple To The Sea	Laura Eves	103
Maya	Ray Dite	104
A Room With A View	A Pearce	104
Growing Up	Carole Buchanan-Brown	105
Night Time	Richard Saunders	106
Waiting	L Wood	106
Foxes At Eastacott	Pamela Gott	107
I Am Never Alone	Patricia Stamp	108
For Hayley's Baptism	Heather Bushnell	108
Better Days	Andy Ryan	109
The Night	Susan Bill	110
Shadows	Martin Makinen	110
Beautiful Somerset	Pat Taylor	111
Bonny Bluebell	Ivy Neville	112
From Within	Natalie Turner	112
Remembering	Val Davies	113
Front Line	Cheryl Poole	114
What Price Victory?	Graham Manuell	114
Thick In Accent Only	Leza Webb	115
Remembrance	Janet R Booth	116
Dogma (Is A Bitch)	Jim Badman	116
Tavy To Tamara	J Wiltshire	117
At The Akbar Night-Club	Edna Carmichael	118
My Friend	June Woodward Martin	119
Royal Visit!	Marie Nanny Dowrick	120
Night	Freda L Norton	121
The Morris Dancers	Brenda Heath	122
Summer In The Forest	Freda Pilton	123
Voices	Des Jones	124
Night Out	B Bisgrove	125

Remembering The Past, Present And Future At A Patchwork Quilt Exhibition	Karen Cook	126
	B M Down	127
Venus	Steve Bradshaw	128
Low Tide	Grace Ayling	129
Dartmoor	M W Cann	130
Wherein Lies Peace	Janet Lang	131
Frome In Bloom	Rose Anderton	132
Dockyard	Emily Wright	133
Problems Defined	Lyn Constantine	134
Cornish Garden	G E M Tamlin	134
November	Freda Pearson	135
Dear Husband	Doreen J Jones	136
To Maia	Ros Ashton Butler	137
Deja-Vu	Nick Stevens	138
Exmoor	Hannah Pratt	138
Sea-Side Train - St Ives 1930's	Humphrey Noall	139
Injustice	Lisa Vanstone	140
Drought's End	P Heppel	141
Missing Pieces	Dawn Coull	142
Genealogy	Lesley Bull	143
River Song	Heather Beer	144
Returning To Dartmoor	Jane Ifold	145
My Silver Shadow	K G Gray	145
Caverns And Caves	Elizabeth Holland	146
Seeing Through	Dauda Zai	147
The Former Yugoslavia	Paul Hilton	148
Sporty Husband, Lazy Wife	Beverly Woollacott	148
Spring	Gwendoline Jacobs	149
Light	Martyn Ingham	150
A Sack Of Jewels	Keith Cozens	151
You!	D L Redman	152
Sweet September	Joan Wakeling	152
Country Bliss	Lynne Betts	153
Withypool Hill	Sandra Kershaw	154

THE FAMILY

The woman was broken
A limb of her life had been taken
And so she felt the pain.
Continuing to exist, function - call it what you will
With a dead heart inside her;
She felt no anger nor bitterness,
But could no longer feel life.

The man, her husband;
Had a lifetime of dreams and feelings shattered,
A mere shadow of his former self
He watched the world go by with lifeless eyes
And felt the pain, he would rather have taken from the child.

They both continued to love
Their remaining children,
But the one that had gone,
They all knew was the favourite,
They felt no envy, nor jealousy;
They too loved the child.

But now she was gone - never returning to enhance the lives
Of the broken mother, shattered father or loving children.
For not one life was taken that summer day
In May, in the country so far away,
But others so close; and some not so close,
Can never again, be the same in life or love
And so the Family, continue, supporting and strengthening
Each other, and perhaps one day
Who knows . . . ?

Annette Furniss

CONTINUO

Within the half-built cities of our dreams
the house of war stands solid,
set between the ministries and the factories,
the knowledge that it holds available to both,
should they wish to hedge a bet.

Inside there are many shining booths and stalls,
the signs shout Power, Status, Fame and Glory,
Just Cause, Approval and Reward,
with price tags reading Misery and injury and Death.
A shadowy, inglorious mart, select for years
but now, again, the queue is round the block.

In other squares and alleyways, entombed in
books and scrolls, scholars and philosophers
seek among the Ozymandian tablets for the key
to all of this.

Must these wild unbridled tyrants forever be
allowed to pull the temples down while both
sides call upon a common God and dreams of
multitudes dissolve once more in sand and mud?

Peter Coxhead

WRITTEN IN BELFAST II

This I have learnt.
That to bury a problem does not solve it.
And to bury a memory does not make it vanish.
A graveyard of problems, old and young lies behind me.
Ghosts and spirits haunt me without respite.
A cemetery of memories assail my mind,
constant reminders of the evils which have been perpetrated,
and of deeds not done which should have been done.

Ken Chalmers

BABY ON THE BEACH

Can you taste the salt as it hangs upon your lips?
Can you see the white spray as it foams around the ships?
Can you smell the seaweed as it piles upon the beach?
Can you touch the pebbles as they tumble out of reach?

Come my little darling, safely take my hand.
Brace your small strong body as we stride across the sand.
Winds might strike and toss us - you are so very small -
But, hand in hand together, neither one of us will fall.

Wilma Jayne Gravenor

THE CANDLE

Hand sheltered candle burning bright,
My steps are guided by your light,
Your flickering flame long shadows throw
As up the stairs to bed I go.

Dancing spectres haunt the walls
Where casted silhouettes do fall!
Intrepid therefore do I go!
Not trusting shadows from your glow!

Your tapered wax extrudes the string
That lights, attracting moth on wing.
Encircling flame it flies around,
Its beating wings the only sound!

Now time has come for my retreat,
I pinch your naked flame at seat,
Then lay long hours wondering where,
That moth has settled from your glare!

Deane Stuart Wynne

COAST WALK

The apple blossom
Beyond the thicket
Reminded me
That once there had been a garden.

A cliff top garden, sloping seawards
Tilled in the rich red earth
Sheltered from prevailing winds
Open to the sun;
A kitchen garden
Repaying the love, the work, the care
With household crops.

The apple blossom
Gentle against the soft hazed blue
Dream drifted its perfume towards the path.

Charmian Astbury

DARK NIGHTS

The darkness of the night
the coldness of the air,
the moon and stars
shining bright,
the moonlit river
and eerie shadows,
that make me shiver
and feel wary,
the beauty of this land
makes me want to stay
forever more,
never having to go away.

Linda Casey

TOWER OF STRENGTH

Counted.
Seventy two,
going up,
coming down,
Always seventy two.

Worn,
rough,
Smooth,
cracked,
loose,
friends.

Going up
light.
Coming down,
dark.
Always seventy two.

Wind,
rain.
Sun,
clouds.
Seagulls,
sounds.

My domain.
Lonely
never,
I'm the
keeper,
The keeper
of the
Light.

Marina Bell

DRECKLY

Cornishmen do it dreckly
or sometimes never at all,
the bathroom would be quite pretty
if only he would finish the wall.

We're building a new kitchen
in a shippon attached to our barn,
he's dug up most of the floor
removed the roof, and 'Oh darn,'

He's off to mend the car,
a good hard worker is he,
but nothing ever gets finished,
'twill be done my dear, dreckly.'

He started digging a pond
be finished by spring I hope,
the dogs keep falling in the hole
and have to be pulled out with rope.

We've been trying to make a garden
planting flowers and the occasional tree,
They've moved quicker down at Heligan,
but ours will be done dreckly.

The roof has now started leaking,
buckets we have galore,
'Don't ee worry my dear,' says he
It saves you washing the floor.

The washing machine needs a washer
now you know I'm not one to moan,
I'll just take the clothes to the river
and beat them with a stone.

Today's our anniversary,
I think of tonight with glee,
But I suppose along with everything else,
I'll be done dreckly.

Jeanne Short

THE SANDPIPER'S LAMENT

Slowly from the north-east comes a chilling sense of Death,
You can feel it in the footholds; you can smell it on the breath.
It pushes under wing-tips, smarms and creeps beneath the skin,
reeks slyly of finales, the dreaded fear you cannot win.

Where has the warmth of August gone? Where fled the short-lived night?
Where gone the mirror surfaces that returned our circling flight?
Where gone the pebbles' safety? Where the boulder's vantage point?
Where goes the summer's confidence, the pair-bond's healing joint?

Will the change to winter quarters bring that longed-for change of heart?
Will a simple switch of scenery re-animation start?
Why must we make this passage, make this wrench with something dear,
with the sacredest of memories left beside this homespun mere?

The lucky ones remaining play in equinoctial rains -
for them no strong temptation to their Italys or Spains;
for them rewarding happiness in fog or sleet or hail,
with the female of the species lying united with the male.

I've no stomach for the journey. Can't we stop the march of time?
Freeze existence in a moment with surrounding beads of rime?
Can't we still the swelling rivers, assuage the raging hills?
Can't we tranquillise the torrents and control the foaming ghylls?

Arnold Bloomer

FOR THE KINGDOM'S SAKE

Though eloquently may I speak,
And educated though I seem,
My walk of faith is mere oblique
Without that love for which most dream.
But filled with simple, caring love
That casts no shadow in its wake,
We happily, unknowing move
And love just for the kingdom's sake.

Andrew Jones

AN ENDING

Turning their backs 'gainst the threatening wind,
The dark veined leaves hung grimly
To the parent branch of the old proud tree,
And asked themselves
Why should we leave thee, stark-branched, you
Who have held us so sturdily,
And allowed us to dance so merrily
All through the Spring and Summer?

Alas, said the proud old tree,
Most things do have an end.
You'll go to nourish Mother Earth
And to her be a friend.
Let winter rant, rave, roar and boom,
I'll stand four-square, and soon
I'll hold more tender leaves to hang as sturdily
And dance as merrily
For another Spring and Summer.

So the tired old leaves drifted softly down,
Gently whispering as they fell,
'Farewell, proud tree, farewell.'

R M Lancaster

THE CHILL OF SILENCE

Wide open spaces,
Requiem for forgotten faces.
Stone floor breeding malaria,
Bleeding a mutilated aria.
Empty expressions staring distorted,
Thought is crushed by dominant torturers.
The smell of stale crawling death,
Bodies stacked by decomposition.
Gas caresses severed senses,
Spinning sickly rank cadavers.

Kendall Lacey

WHY CRY YOU STILL?

Oh worrying boy, atop the hill,
How can you cry, how can you still?
Across the bay you see the past,
You see the fears and how they last.
You see the sand, the sea below,
How daily to, how daily fro,
Across the bay lies the heart -
The end to tears, a brand new start.

Oh worrying boy, atop the hill,
You've swallowed the hard and bitter pill,
Thought that life could only be
What your parents and friends made you see.
And looking for that strength you've found
No strong support, no land that's sound
- Forgive me, boy, atop the hill,
See I now why cry you still.

Dean Smith

RAINBOW

A Rainbow
Defending darkness, defending light;
Without the rain, the sun,
There can be no Arch;
A young woman
At the kitchen sink
Up to her elbows
In stain-remover and starch;
Sees its colours, its height, its span
Looks at it, declaring: 'I am
Certain,'
Reaches up, pushing further
The curtains
Open.

Nicola van Koutrik

MOOR

Vast granite monarch, rising in protest,
Struggle for freedom from the clinging bracken,
Purple-crowned, mist clad, menacing mighty!
One hundred vassals call across thy realm.
The Moor is their home -
They must defend it against the rash invaders,
They must repel the vile advancing hordes,
Sending them back, nevermore to return.
Preserve the great kingdom, let it remain unsullied.
They call it progress; let us have none of it.
Let them yield place to thy Jurassic eminence.
Travel they may, but not by these ways.
They shall not pass in their reeking chariots
Spreading pestilence with their foul fumes.
No share for them in this jewel in thy crown.

Ben Morland

AN AIRFIELD AT WAR

Bleak, cold and windy days,
Pilots clad in passed down leather jackets
Gathered round the NAFFI stand,
Hands clutching warm mugs
As snowflakes tumble down onto
Runways below.

Scramble, scramble.
The distinctive sound of propellers turning,
Chocks away.
Another crew departs, another fails to return.

Maybe more lost, who knows.
Maybe more won, who knows.
Till the sound of grumbling engines
Floats into the ear, or doesn't,
Over the speckled trees.

Matthew Turpin

PICTURE BOX CRIME

Slack suit, gruff hoods,
Yellow door reveals a scene,
Step back, merit thoughts,
Unity entwined, lovers guilt,
Knotted limbs splayed.
Defiant mimes unveil
Open heart, shuttered peace.
Neon halos binding
Cataract innocence.
Ivy portal exhausts, only
Wrought forms wrapped
By cloth ears, left.

Matthew Barnes

RAIN RAIN GO AWAY

It's rained every day for the past three weeks
I've a hole in my roof and lots of leaks.
The garden is soggy, and my feet sink deep
Whenever I venture off paving or street.

You'd imagine now that February's out
March would arrive without too much clout.
You'd be fooling yourself, and me as well,
Because March arrived, and it's sheer hell.

There's rain and sleet, but make no mistake
We'll have gales and thunder arrive in their wake.
As for April, May and June
If they arrive tomorrow it cannot be too soon.

One thing that helps me, and you as well
The weather's foul at the moment, but this I foretell
Unless something's amiss in the heavens above
Spring will arrive balmy breezes and flowers
Followed by summer's hot sun, gentle showers.

If this is not so, I don't know about you
I know what I'll do and I'll do it soon
Pack up my bags and leave for the Moon!

Constance Burniston

DROWNING

Now I see you through the ocean of water between us.
I reach out and cannot touch the hair that was once as molten copper in my hands.
My limbs are cold and leaden, and irresistible currents are sweeping me from you.
The submarine landscape is suffused with the sapphire of your eyes, and I am sinking.
I am perpetually drowning.

You are beyond the surface, turning to the summer-green land,
scattering, as you go, soft scarlet rose-petals on the water.
Straining, I raise my lips to one single petal.
And then fall back to the cold embrace of the clinging wrack,
the insidious, embalming grip of endless days.
All dying away to the dark, seditious cave of sleep.

G R Sowden

I KNOW A MAGIC LAND

Where the rainbow meets the sea
And the dolphins leap and play,
Where seabirds call
And strong winds blow
There's a land, part real, part fey.

The foaming surf on the sand,
Below the softly waving trees,
Set in summer sun
And azure skies
And the warm, caressing breeze.

To walk the paths of old
The saints, and smuggler's way,
Through moorland wild
O'er cliff and cove
To seek some sheltered bay.

Churchmen read their office,
Ancient stones stand strong
'Gainst mighty winds
And clashing waves
This - *Kernow's* magic song.

Hilary Greensmith

THE MOURNING

The morning stood back,
Trying to appear indifferent,
To carry on with its other business,
But I could tell
That it could not concentrate.

The sun staggered across
And was hazy with the strain
Of looking through my greasy windows
When I appeared not to be.

My Servant fetched my toast
And pulled up a seat,
Placed my provisions before me
And began, meekly, to eat.
The morning thought it was me,
But I was looking
And so was he,
While the Servant (as usual), drank my tea.
It has more eyes than I,
And averts which ever one I see.
But I know the others probe
Both gently and sadly at me.

I knew the morning was afraid,
Compelled to hide behind a haze
Of life and endless machinery;
He was dead, and fearfully still
As I placed my cup on the window sill.
My Servant dressed and washed and left,
And the morning, sombre still, he wept.

Anthony Lane

NO SHIPS AT FRENCH WEIR

The river
flows through French Weir,
somebody there
is feeding ducks.

Where the tide crawls in
over glass
and seagulls broken cries,
notes in a bottle
describe the life
of a man who cannot swim.

I never claimed to be
the sinking of the Titanic
or
the phantom Marie Celeste.
The ship,
it never comes in,
it's drifting,
ghostly and deserted.

Where the tide crawls in
over broken glass,
will you love me as I drown,
and we are both,
at last, too late?

On the river near French Weir
bobs a bird
without
a
voice.

Nick Haines

IN LOVING MEMORY OF THE OLD FIDDLER!

Being an old fiddle
On which many a good tune could still be played,
I mourn the passing of the old fiddler.
Did he run out of rosin?
Did he break his bow?
Or perhaps he just didn't give a pluck any more.
I'm not asking for Bach!
An Irish gig would do.
Just to feel a bow across my strings again.
Even a good tuning up would be better than nothing.
A fiddle that no one plays is just firewood!

Naomi Wheelwright

BEFORE DAWN ON CORNISH MOORS

There is no wind along the darkened land;
No star reflected in the sea's quiet streams.
There is no light along the shadowy sand.
On the high moors alone, the pale moon gleams.

O silent sea! Vast silence of the night.
On hollow valley and cold dew-drenched lawn;
Those distant beams of frozen silver light
Are lost in darkness deepest before dawn.

Lost! - So the loved are lost. World lonely, wide;
Hearts ache when day is bitter, winter grey.
Immense the strength of time's relentless tide;
Of storms that whirled our once proud youth away.

Yet, at the heart of darkness, calm, since night
Is given for sleep, for dreams, for earth to be
In dawns innumerable new made, made light;
Paths of pure gold across the uncharted sea.

Diana Momber

PORTHMEOR BEACH

Wow!
What a scene:
Cascading water
Falls between unusual
Rock formations.
Wide curve of golden sand
Before us;
Curve and taper of architecture
Behind us.
Surfers and artists
Parade the mind
Porthmeor Beach,
Wow what a surprise!

Alex Langstone

HISTORY GOING

What are they missing down in the soil
As they blast about, radios on
What are they missing as they madly toil?

They are missing the history that lies in the ground
Claypipes, horseshoes, pottery of all sorts
Spanners and china are all to be found.

One wonders who used these things of old
The age of them and their uses and
Oh! What interesting stories could be told.

Will these pieces of history survive this battering, never
With deep ploughs, de-stoners and power harrows
We are losing them for ever.

G James

CAMELOT

It is sold as mystery, beauty and purity,
Bought in longing for treasure, peace and lucidity.
A temporary escape from their lives,
All summer weather and joy it provides.
Ancient environment, mother of my history,
My place of knowing, an abandonment of secrecy.

This rural is a collage of experiences,
Playing, teasing and awakening my senses.
Its smell is damp, warm, something allusive,
Its taste fresh, naturally seductive,
The vision always enamoured by those it touches.
I welcome this simplicity and what it teaches.

Celebration of past, progressive in regression
Joining body, soul, earth, a physical connection.
Released in this place, my spirit is freed,
Drifting with the clouds, a scent on the breeze.
This county a catalyst for real emotion,
I'm encompassed in the inspirational potion.

When this abode of expression becomes a memory
I know I will attempt to recall my history,
Sounds of the wind hindered only by space,
The gentle rain tantalising my face,
The sun will set leaving an image of clemency,
A warmth to enjoy, an escape from reality.

L Faulkner

THE KEY

Inside my grandma's house she kept a little key
The key unlocked a door to a room I'd longed to see
So once when I was staying there, I found the key by chance
It was then that I decided to take a little glance

So when my Gran went shopping, my chance had come at last
I put the key into the lock and walked into the past
The room was full of all kinds of antique toy
I guessed they had been Grandma's, they were her pride and joy

China dolls looked at me all dressed in silk and lace
All Granny's clothes from long ago, were packed inside a case
But so intrigued was I in this room of many treasures
That I forgot if I was caught, Gran would resort to drastic measures

I had always been forbidden to ever go within
She told me if I entered, she'd consider it a sin
Then I heard a creaking beyond the door outside
I knew I had to face her, I hadn't time to hide

She sent me to my room and deprived me of my dinner
She also said she thought I was a proper little sinner
It's all forgotten now of course and I'm a Gran myself
I also have a little key that I keep upon a shelf

I inherited Granny's house, when she passed away
And I've kept that room exactly as I'd found it on that day
But instead of hiding Granny's joys as she had always done
I let the children play in there and have a bit of fun

But when I see that little key sitting on the shelf
I think about the day I had played in there myself
I never knew why Gran had hidden her past away
And I never will as she isn't here to say.

T Tucker

SUNSTARVED

Sun drenched bay:
High and higher
Bright white light
Climbs above the
Clumps of snow
Mountain clouds.
Rays strike down,
Sparkle broad on
Mirror sea.
Thousands of tiny
Moving glimmers
Encompass a lone
Boat in their expanse.
Chimney potted roof
Tops are silhouettes
Against the brightness,
Blue sky each side
Softens the eye-hurting
Awesome early morning
Scene which fills my
Heart with light.
I breathe it into my
Sunstarved winter
Crestfallen body.

Susan Burgess

THE BEST IN LIFE

People find it difficult to understand,
Why money and possessions are not our God,
Why we've never strove for these,
But we're happy in the path we've trod.

We love the changing colours of the trees,
The sound of waves lapping on the shore,
The crackling of a log fire,
These cost nothing and mean much more.

It doesn't cost to see a brilliant sunset at night,
A bird carrying things to its nest,
An early morning mist rising from the ground,
To let the earth breathe, these things to us are the best.

Jeanette Harris

ON THE OCCASION OF OUR SON'S WEDDING

In January ninety-four the ring was on display.
The months ahead saw love just grow.
They looked toward this day.

That year just came and went it seems, priorities quite torn.
With jobs and flats and church life too, another year was born.

In January ninety-five, Wendy exclaimed, 'This year!'
The weeks reducing one by one, today was drawing near.

The weeks were soon reduced to days, frustration too crept in.
Plans all achieved, just left to wait, a husband now to win.

For Jon, the time has just flown by amidst the youth work strain,
The dishes and the washing too, all water down the drain!

So now we've come to share your joy with family and friend.
Now we've *two* daughters and a son. Our joy will have no end.

'Marriage takes three, God, you and me,' so says a card you've had.
Our prayer would very simply be, may *His* heart make yours glad.

Paul Langford

DEFLATED AT THE EISTEDDFOD

At Eisteddfods I've always been happy
those lilting voices so clear
with songs and poetry so tender
making memories of childhood so dear.

The dancing, the costumes, the language
the tempo, the colours, the pride,
who could not enjoy these festivities
and put all one's worries aside.

But I have to relate I was saddened
by a man sitting next to me
who was noisily slurping a yoghurt
whilst a Soprano was on her top C

'I'm here to enjoy the Eisteddfod
not listen to you sucking food.
Do you think you could eat more quietly
and not be so blatantly rude?'

'Enjoy your Eisteddfod' he quietly sneered
'Whilst inferring I eat like a vulture,
but just bear in mind my superior friend
that my yoghurt needs a *live* culture.'

W E Dinneen

CASTLE BEACH

Sea nymphs rise
then fall,
a million wings
tempered by silver rain.
Waves break
to escape
the ignescent magic
of these fiery maidens.

On a nearby hillside
a leaping tree god
is caught in mid-flight,
embalmed in brackish wind.
At its feet
a cluster of golden flowers
burn in the April sun.
Holding a constant vigil
for this tortured soul,
maliciously teased
by the sea's
seductive charms.

S Winfield

YESTERDAY

Yesterday memories
Caught in faded photos,
Yesterday faces,
Forgotten or nameless,
Yesterday smiles
Shining through time,
Yesterday places
Blurred in the mind,
Yesterday playtime,
Kiss chase,
      'You're caught!'
Hopscotch,
      Time warp,
Yesterday dreams
Of yesterday scenes,
Yesterday lost,
Forever.

Lindsay Atfield

DROUGHT 1995

It's the longest hottest heatwave since seventeen twenty seven
Farmers are getting angry, and praying up to heaven
Next winter's feeds are being used, the grass is burnt and brittle
Drinking troughs are empty, rivers and streams have very little
The westcountry dowser's are working at great speed
to locate the boreholes for some of the people's needs.
Listen to the forecast, no rain, what a pain, another hot day
reservoir's low, here we go, standpipes we hear them say.
More holiday makers coming down, but to the sea they duck and dive
It really helps to freshen up, after a tiresome but worthwhile drive.
In Cornwall they are thinking of drilling deep down in undergrown sites
for vast quantities of pure water to stop the watermen's fight.
The Firemen are at their wits end, vast fires are tinder dry
fires that creep relentlessly as they sweep towards the sky.
Shrubs and flowers are withering, tree roots are really parched dry
people restricted of watering, enough to make them cry.
Water has no taste or smell, which we cannot do without
we realise how precious it is now we've got a drought.
Now they are doing a rain dance, by an American Cherokee
beyond belief the magic worked, everyone's dancing with glee.

M M R Greenaway

UNTITLED

You're the air I breathe,
the next step forward into the freshness,
The sky kissing the granite, touching the sea.
Your land, my land
Moorland, mining,
Clayland, grassland, all intertwining
to give us Kernow, to give us living,
The envied life, of the hopeful.

Gerry Doe

HORN OF A BULL, HOOF OF A HORSE, SMILE OF A SAXON

At home branches reach up into mist
like mangled hands of Celts they could not quell.
Talons tear at the dancing air clawing and
slashing those memories of my Devonshire boy,
which molest me like gorse on the beacon scratching.

Wind menaces my flesh like a rapist's angry mouth;
even its salt tastes of you my Saxon love.
You thrust a colony in my heart.
You ate at its perimeters
Almost conquering the coast of my being.

Upon black granite cliff I envisaged sea-subtle powers;
saffron locks still break upon your forehead
soothing as coves below; your eyes
horizonless; deceitful as the Atlantic
enticed me over the edge.

It took a traveller's eye to see
you were no ocean but a channel
I was stuck on your sandbanks.
Now your shallow words are lost here
Kernow shields me from your invading touch.

I bathe in the spirit of the bards
who with their magic have summoned
a man in a kilt pulling me from the sand.
The strength in his accent and in his sword arm
that holds me like rock
signals the oppressor is weak
and I at last at home.

Anna Forsyth

ELMER'S MUSIC

Hands raw with the milking in the frost at dawn,
hair unkempt, and trousers sagging,
he trudged, late, to his desk to doze in a haze
through the mewling melodramatic maze,
the daily mouthing of meaningless learning.
Then, through the clouds of misconception,
two words he heard, 'Well done! That's good.'
He had made an astonishing calculation
that two and two more were suddenly four.

That day his whole world gained a new dimension.
Four places he knew where the sundew grew;
four speckled blue eggs lay in his thrush's nest;
a brood of four skylarks were concealed in the sedge.
The vixen's four secrets would be safely guarded
beneath the dark hollies at the forest's edge.
Rainbow colours flashed through his night
when his brown owl hooted twice times two.
Through the attic window he could name four stars
shining only for him with an intimate light.
He would walk through the churchyard four feet taller,
no longer afraid of the shade of the yew.
'My life is good,' he said, 'for I did not know what I knew.'

R Midwinter

THE GARDEN

The garden, green and gracious in the early dawn,
The small birds come to bless the earth
The flowers bloom round me as I move
To touch the grass bedecked in summer dew.

The shadows lengthen as the daylight goes
The golden lily and crimson rose

Begin to close their petals for the night
And now I learn to wait with quiet delight
For evensong that chants beyond the church.

The God of nature came to me with love
And gentle creatures brought me new delight
As slowly stars and moonlight shine so bright
To deck the sky with glory for the night.

Marcella Pellow

MIRROR MIRROR ON THE WALL . . . WHO . . .

Face, and forehead creasing,
Nose large, eyes now dimming,
Mouth small, teeth showing wear.
There the chin, dark and bare.
Neck scraggy, tells of time.
Muscles never in prime.
And, beneath head balding,
a brain random rambling.
Heart offbeating strangely.
Lungs struggling gamely.

So I watch, watch life, daily enjoying.
Age has wearied, the years are condemning.
With thoughts still young, desires out of tune.
So dream, I tell myself, and in dreams immune.
Smile, as the world goes by, developing,
enjoying itself, and madly changing,
for better, for worse, forever, because
until I say farewell, this was my life that was.

How futile? A waste of time?
Was it? Is it? But not to me!

N G Cooper

THE SILENCE AT COME-TO-GOOD

O clear and undivided is the word we seek,
Rising from the Silence of the faithful few.
Clear and undivided is the knowledge of the Lord
When meeting here we listen for His still small voice.
Under this high thatched havening roof the Friends
Come to a greater good than others know.
Curious explorers seeking the picturesque
Find in this quiet lane beside a farm
A sudden well of peace, a witness to their Faith
Who in the past withstood the scorn, the lash
Of Puritanic laws, incarceration for their pleas:
George Fox and Loveday Hambly, Ann Upcott . . .

O hallowed Come-to-Good, or Cwm-ty-Coit,
Valley of the House in the Woods: it comes to this,
That humankind must seek Him as it can,
In myriad ways, in song and prayer and thought,
In Eucharist and sermon, confession, holy books . . .
Yet the kernel of all faith is surely silence.
Until the world is shut out, and the fog
Of its coarse pleasures can recede, we cannot hear:
Until we bow in quietude and thrust all words
And argument away, we never shall receive
The Logos latent in our inmost souls.

O clear and undivided is the Word
That rises from the Silence of these few.

(George Fox, the Quaker leader, was imprisoned in 1655 in Launceston Castle, for publishing a manifesto. Loveday Hambly of Tregongreeves was also imprisoned for her beliefs. Ann Upcott of St Austell was put in the stocks for mending a garment on Sunday)

Donald Rawe

THE COURSE TO END ALL COURSES

        So you want to be a writer
        This is how you must begin
        It's ideal for budding talent
        Please do send the coupon in.

        If you want to sell your efforts
        Either prose or all in verse
        Send a fiver for our brochure
        You could do a whole lot worse.

We pride ourselves on guidance for beginners
You don't even have to know the way to spell
We know that we are really on a winner
We are hiring out word processors as well.

We've got publishers of books right in our pocket
We've got editors that eat out of our hand
We use the old-boy network, no don't knock it
And we take them out to luncheon in the strand.

We advise you on your style and presentation
And will help you make a fortune without fuss
We give guidance about writing for the masses
Did you know that Barbara Cartland came to us.

Now we're really not in this to make a profit
We work hard for every penny that we earn
If you think that money's vulgar, then come off it
Kindly sign enclosed bank debit and return.

You are now at the beginning of your lustrum
At your disposal is our limitless know-how
We thank you for your very valued custom
Lesson one is in the post to you right now.

Nora Mostyn-Bond

THE GIRO

The piece of paper with my name upon it falls silently onto the mat.
it is opened with formidable fingers whilst the merry-round begins,
reciting its for this and for that,
It sits a while on the mantle-piece until the pain inside subsides,
the relentless pain which remains and drains faced once again with
how to make it stretch . . . go further than I know it can,
Waves of turmoil spread throughout, numbing then succumbing until at
last they wan, acceptance takes over, anger increases with the
demanding question . . . Why do I have to live this way, never, ever ceasing,

The question is answered within a short time . . . I am made to suffer
for not having a job . . . made to feel as though I have committed a crime,
made to feel guilty and called a scrounger, shamed for excepting others
hard earned moneys . . . a lounger in their nest-eggs,
Pride becomes as a dodo, obsolete, forever gone and always a fear of
what one may become, the children's eyes say it all, the blankness
and confusion, lost dreams, lost hope, no way out at all,

Again I take a look, the giro beckons to be spent, choke down held
in emotions which are never, ever spent, for the door to them is
always ajar as like a prison cell and I the prisoner with no hope of
finding a key, but from the loneliness and poverty strength rises its head,
giving fuel to recover . . . to stand tall and not fall back into the large black
hole shared by many others, also *cared for* by those who say they
understand our needs, our wants, who rule *our land* . . .
. . . And . . . Our stomachs.

Kathleen Schmidt

AUTUMN MIST IN ROBOROUGH

Cat-like, curling, honey white,
The morning mist seeps through the trees.
The village sleeps beneath a damp-quiet quilt,
Dream shapes in a dawn frieze.

Shadowy swallows on wires
Whisper of distant, burning plains.
They will be gone soon. Phantoms of passage,
Scything through autumn rains.

Magic mist, weaver of dreams,
Holding Apollo's warmth at bay.
Then softly, silently on morning wings
To gently glide away.

Diana H Adams

REMEMBERING

Whatever happened to the good old days, when a knees up
                                        was considered fun,
The good old days, when we stuck together, World War 1 and 2
                                        were won.
The Pearly Kings, the Pearly Queens, the Londoners sing along,
                                        dance and care,
The heart of the country, Londoners proud, would always
                                        give and share.
We served our King and country - everyone special in their own way,
The good old days will stay with us, for we're proud, that is our way.
The family charabanc outings, delayed at the out-break of the war,
The blitz, air-raid warnings, then inside the Morrison or Anderson we saw.
Our Land Army, the Home Guard they worked and served to help us all,
Throughout the war, the bombings, partings, loss, Londoners still stood tall.
A great occasion 50 years on - when VE day arrived,
And remembered those who lost their lives, by us that have survived.
I'm a Londoner, and proud - yes, proud to talk about my past,
I'm a Londoner, have memories, many tales, that forever will last.
Down to earth are we, stick together, help out when someone is in need,
I'm proud to be a Londoner - yes - I'm very proud indeed.

Irene Mooney

OUT ON THE MARSHES

Marshland as far as the eye can see.
The sun's in the west and she's beckoning me
to the gold-green pools and the tall reeds sighing.

Then go, my child, but don't stay late
where the wind plays the pipes of the iron gate
to the rustling reeds and the curlew calling.

The sun sinks down like stone in the mire,
the path runs down and the reeds grow higher
in the still, dark pools of the daylight's dying.

Fingers of vapour begin to tease
and twine and tangle; the dying breeze
just a faint unease in the reed-bed stirring.

Dropped like a twig by the daylight's ebb,
caught like a fly in the spider's web
of the rising mist and the darkness falling.

J A Collinge

THE CALLING

This is my element
Walking free beneath the trees
Breathing darkness.
Yet day-blind I shadow forth
Tentative form, ambiguous truth,
Possibility of the undeduced.
Here, shedding self, I become
Cold apple clenched and pure,
Silver equipoise of dew,
Night-jar, toad or troubadour,
A shade of night by night consumed.

Hannah Julian

THE WHITE GIANTS OF GARLAND CROSS

To me you are a thing of beauty
To others a blot upon the landscape
You stand at Garland Cross for all the world to view.
Your tall thin bodies have no shape.
They fitted you not with two strong arms but three.
How quickly you all turn, to North, East, South and West
Whichever way the wind do blow.
But in the heat of the sun, you hardly move, or
When the snow lay thick upon the ground.
But given a gale you nearly take off.
You give off a sound just like a whine, could it be
You are lonely giants with no-one to care or praise
the work you do.
When all around mad voices can be heard
'Take they there things down today,' they cry.
But we in Cornwall, do know our folklore
For it was told, long ago in Arthur's time
That giants would again come back to Cornwall
And sure enough them ere.
'But what are'm for?' we ask.
Some'd say they help light our homes and towns
But I'm like the rest,
I'm not so sure.
We shall have to wait a while
Cause they there giants have yet to speak.

Joan Hewitt

JANUARY

The bells have rung their welcome and are still.
        The polished stars are diamond bright and hard.
The ewes, dark grey against the light grey hill,
        shift restlessly. Across the cobbled yard

from where I stand, the pampered, patient cows
        (so sweet their breath despite the midden stink)
deep in straw's comfort chew their cud, or drowse,
        or slurp in drinking-bowls, neck chains a-clink.

Weightless, the barn owl glides in silent flight,
        a brief white shadow through engulfing black,
shredding the stagnant silence of the night
        with his keen shriek. Then silence trickles back.

The bells have rung their welcome and are dumb.
        Silent the pub's loud laughter, boist'rous cheers.
Quiet through the night another year has come
        fresh with bright hopes - like all the other years.

Martin Summers

VILLAGE IN NOVEMBER

The bonfire that sat astride the village green lies dead.
Charred embers laced with frost where once the flames did laugh and dance.

Cottages with smoking stacks, fireside chairs stuffed full with men,
And pink faced wives and lazy dogs,
And inglenook packed high with logs.

Idle cart; redundant plough, pervading smell of apple bough.
Potting shed with frozen lock, measured sound of brass top clock.
Murmuring kettle soon to boil, destined someone's sleep to spoil.

Ray Calaz

GOD'S LOVE

May God's love surround you,
As you go from day to day.
May his blessings manifest themselves,
As you travel on your way.

The wonders of the World around you,
Are bounteous to behold.
From the majestic splendour of the trees.
To the mighty power of the seas.

The azure blue sky and beaches of gold,
The daunting cliffs, and the caves beneath.
With every pebble, rock and reef,
And their mysteries to enfold.

From the tiniest insect, to the mightiest beast,
Each is God's own creature,
To say the very least,
And each is to his own, with Mother Nature.

The myriads of flowers,
With their colours of every hue,
The lakes and streams and rivers,
So much to captivate your view.

Don't waste time with trivialities,
Take time to look around you.
And feel the peace and wonder,
As God's love surround you.

A Roberts

FAIRIES

There's a place in the garden
Where all the fairies go
You may not believe in fairies
but there are such things you know
it is their little meeting place
on every afternoon
they dance when the sun is up
until they see the moon
and when they see the moon up so high
the fairies disappear up into the sky

Leanne Taylor (10)

STONES THROWN AWAY

I looked upon the city lights, across
Ten thousand lonely graves
Came in search of memories
For which my heart still craves

Standing in the graveyard
Surveying all the stones
Now they are your castles
Now they are your thrones

A mound of earth, beckons a body to enclose
Whilst on guard o'er soldiers' graves
                stands a pure red rose
Its scent lingers longer than his memory
                all but dead
A lone man salutes you with both heart and head
Amongst the trees sway daffodils
Dwarf conifers shade tulips
His memory strives to exist
Another day passes and his memory slips.

G S Riggs

BLUE TEARS I CRY ON WEDNESDAY

A broken smile
To wake the day
No laughing bones
Along the way
A king
A queen
The jokers pair
A broken moon
In darkness where?

A broken heart
Till death the day
Thou darkness stand
His birth I pray
The sun
The moon
The natural pair
A broken word
The guilty fair

A broken peace
The crimson dead
With dampen sweat
Upon my head
A God
A man
The foolish pair
A broken world
And no-one cares

Lee Robinson

MY SISTER HAS LONG HAIR

their house
I'll take the rooms upstairs

there's nowhere like
Keats house
bricks of serenity
in Hampstead

holding thoughts,
trills, notes erupting
in Keats backyard

a whole expansion
poured on page
held by
soft tremors, incandescent
with rage

in these rooms of graces
desires
affectionate stirrings
love held sway

nightingale never
knew
its offspring would
renew
poets alike
to revel
in it its own delight

Maureen Given

A CHILD'S MEMORY

I remember the churchyard down by the canal
And wandering along the towpath
under a dark velvet canopy, speckled with glitters of gold.

I remember - I was not so very old.
The shadows cast by the gravestones, jutting starkly into
                                                       the moonlight
The ripples of luminosity on the black, black water
A moribund ribbon
And I quivered to the echoing hollowness of the wasteland
stretching wide, the other side.
With wisps of palpitating mists drifting in the night
I was so sad
And anxious for my plight
The street lights, dimly showing through the spaces
And whispering in the cracks and crevices of the knot of
houses beyond the church
Which stood gaunt, and overpowering
Towering into the depths of the twinkling sky
I remember looking up - it seemed so very high
The steeple pierced the heavens
Such a Holy place, and I, a child, was in disgrace

The headstones were the forward guard
The houses, the rear guard
The canal, the moat
And raging souls moaned with the wind on the waste ground
Mustering for attack.

I was lost, and couldn't go back.
I remember climbing through the fence and praying
Saying sorry for being rude
Promising to know my place
To be more full of grace.

Pat W Hillyer

WINTER

Snowflakes falling from the air,
Crystal patterns carpeting the ground like silk,
Walking through the soft snow,
Crunching ice.
Suddenly, foggy mist,
Blindly finding the way like being in a
dream you can't get out of.
Soon it lifts,
Coldness, dampness in the air,
Biting winds,
Hands clenched in pockets,
Hurrying home to a warm, crackling fire.

Natalie J Barker

MAX

You are a soft warm wrap
Lying curled upon my lap.
What are you dreaming?
Tail softly moving,
Whiskers all of a twitch.

Your presence is here in the house,
Frightenly clear to that mouse.
You pounce and you claw, and so it seems
That mouse is not only in dreams
You wake with a me-ow and a stretch.

Oh, Maxi, your eyes golden lights,
Your fur, soft and black as the night.
A lick and a kiss for me is alright.
But that mouse, better stay out of sight
With neither a scamper or squeak!

Lynda Callard

SCHOOLBOY

Satchel on back, a shining face
Shoes on feet not even laced
Hat on head, back to front
Rise each morning with a grunt
Gnash his teeth, won't comb his hair
Lost his homework, do not care.

In the classroom have a ball
Draw nude pictures on the wall
Never ready when you call
From the highest branches fall
Schooling, has no time for any
Rather go fishing with young Lenny.

Tells you proudly the latest craze
Mind in whirl, such a maze
His school days such a waste
Little girls would rather chase
Many an hour in mischief lost
Must be chief, likes to boss.

Face of innocent, chubby red cheeks
All your time that schoolboy seeks
Gives the neighbours a real treat
On tin cans in garden beat
Whistle off beat, tiny marching feet
While awake, none shall sleep.

Face light up when he's praised
When he's naughty all hell raised
Clothes in tatters, seen better days
That smiling face has winning ways
Charm the birds off the trees
Only good in him will see.

P Powell

BEAUTY

Folds of skin
Growing smaller and more fragrant towards the heart,
But gradually opening, to disclose
Your prized possession.
You blush!
Your face is petal tinted -
A little lilac haze.

Standing alone
You drink from the glass.
I cannot believe that you,
Now at your prime,
Will soon die.
Your faded petals and drooping figure
Will be cast out.

Perhaps next year, that same bush
Will yield
Another rose,
As well formed as you.
Sweetening the air outside
As you do here.
I have found beauty in you.
Go now,
And share your wealth with others.

Jill Allen

NO TEARS FOR ME

Don't cry for me
I shall not see
Those tears you shed for me.
No matter the expanse of time I could not
Hide the hurt inside.
So cry no tears for me.

No good to say it's gone, it's over
To me it was as yesterday.
Something like that for me would never go away.
So cry no tears for me.

The hurt I hide
Will stay inside,
So cry no tears for me.

Don't cry for me unless you see
To me the hurt was real
No matter how the time went by
It would to me be real,
Unless you see
Then cry no tears for me.

Mabel Mills

MASK

Like a favourite toy,
Lost and briefly longed for,
You turned up, years too late.

We still fitted like an old boot;
The utterly familiar heaviness
Of your careless arm on my shoulder as we walked;
Did you notice any slight discomfort?
Could you feel pinpricks in the platitudes?

We laugh, masking ourselves.
We have different skin now,
New hair, new bones.
Time heals by replacing the parts.
Levels of reality, but how to scale them?

Frances Thompson

A PRISON BOY

A prison boy came home one day
to find his truelove gone away.
If you repent a life of crime
go back to prison and do your time.
So back to prison he did go
and in his cell, he cried like hell.
In the morning screws around him,
Dead, and in his hand a letter read.
Dig my grave
Dig it deep
Lay red roses at my feet
and on my chest, tattoo a dove
And tell the world he died for love.

Sebina Clare Heffernan

AUTUMN BREEZE

Soft blows the heather that grows on the hill,
Like the feathered foam of a purple sea;
Rustled by the blustery autumn chill
Of the ocean wind weaving wearily.

Over the misty seas it breathes
Its fresh heather scent on the curling waves.
Slowing, gently, it writhes and wreathes
In the salty air of the booming caves.

On the utmost watery wall of these
It faints and falls on the bubbling stone.
So ends the life of the heather-borne breeze
As it dies with a silent whisper, alone.

Anne H Brooks

THE STONE

He's like a stone
Thrown into water
Causing ripples for me.
It could only be a small pebble
But the impact will cause a wave,
Why is the stone being thrown?
Is the stone-thrower not giving up?
I feel paralysed
I can't stop the stone being thrown
I can't stop the ripples
The stone can never absorb the water
So why are they thrown together?
It doesn't know that the ripples
Are killing me.
The stone-thrower strikes again
Not knowing the water is happy still
But the water wants to be disturbed
It longs for the day when the stone is thrown
For the very last time
Only then will the water and the stone be happy.

Victoria Pretty (16)

SECRET

My sister's got a secret,
She's told my mum and dad.
The fact that she hasn't told me
Has made me rather mad.
She's written it in her diary,
She's written it in her books.
I know it's something to do with me -
I can tell that by her looks.

Caroline Tiernan-Locke (10)

AMELIA'S CAT

Amelia Brown
Went into town
To buy a new felt hat
But, she did not know, that
She was followed by her cat

She tried on hats
That looked like thatch
One had a veil, even a tail
And was coloured very pale
Just like a glass of Ale.

The hat was heavy
It felt like a jelly
And wobbled and wobbled about
She started to pout
And then hurried out

Amelia Brown
Got back from town
There sat that naughty cat
As well I did not buy that hat
For it looked just like my cat

Jean Bitmead

LADY 'O'

In the hush of dark, when breath was quiet
A smooth and fragrant dream had I
With tender touch, you had become my love
Deep in your spirit burned part of me

My chest did pillow your maiden face
With locks of silk my fingers caressed
Your lips they did moisten, my very soul
Tears that tasted: honey-rose and dew

Never had I so warmed to the night
For your words came reaching to me
How I longed to tell you of this, my love
Yet, afraid to say more than was wanting

But enough, lest now I call out your name
'Tis surely too late for you to learn
Of the passions that soar within this heart
And of a fool that yearns for you. . .

My wondrous Lady 'O'.

P A Windsar

GOLDEN DAYS

Golden gorse covered cliffs
Granite rocks sparkle with ore
Flume covered waves
Lap gently on the shore.

Thrift covered dunes
Echo to the skylark cry
A gentle blue sky overhead
Cotton wool clouds float by.

Heather covered moors
Where ponies graze
Tiny creatures in their nests
Amidst the field of maize.

Snowdrops show their pearly heads
Daffodils like sunlight gleam
Hyacinth green tips appear
Soon to open as in an artist's dream.

Lydia Stanton

FORCE 10 IMMINENT

From the brow the view was January grave
Ilfracombe's back door closed to no nonsense
waves.
Like heavy artillery hauled ashore, mortuary
slabs of ocean shovelled around the rocks
dark roots.

Like flak, parochial gulls soared answering back
authentic semi quavers, no ashtip mimicry
The gale in a trench coat crowds empty doorways . . .

At Mullacott Cross, a lean wind campaigns
blitzkrieg strategy, gusts drive around the
Traffic Island . . . Stravinsky plagiarised.

Devon farms abseiled to the valley floor
sheep on the high moor . . . shawled . . . granny faced
Hebrews called -
Piloting my thoughts into a surfeit of solitude.
Girth of the sky now sagging
We hurried for home
Lundy . . . Plain . . . Ominous.

David Dudley

UNTITLED

The vision I see is a real one
With my back to the hills,
and my eyes to the sea.
Man has witnessed its force,
Yet harvested its essence.
Its might has its very own history,
And our future in its tide.

D A Russell

SADLY MISSED BY ALL

Why did it happen,
Why happen to me,
Why not someone else,
I don't deserve this,
It's not as if I did anything wrong,
Why should I be punished,
I want to get on with my life,
I want to live again,
I want the pain to go away,
Why can't I turn back the clock,
Just to say goodbye,
To hear your voice,
And see you one more time,
I long to see you,
For you to be back here,
You may be happy where you are,
I wish you never went,
Why does life have to end,
Why couldn't you stay here,
To see us all grow up,
To make sure we don't go wrong,
I hope we shall meet again,
In another life, I don't know,
You shall never be forgotten,
You are sadly missed by all,
With all my love and all my heart,
I will always remember you.

Emma Francis

KILLING ANGELS

I dreamed I saw the Holy May
A-sit a seat on high
Fine robes adorned his girded loin
a glint a-gleamed his eye
And thunder raged and lightning flashed
As trembled voice said I
I have to ask a question, Lord
Why do the animals die?

I love the lambs in green fields play
The ponies down they lie
The goats they graze their days away
Their young for milk they cry
And cows caress their little ones
Beneath the big blue sky
The wind blows free forever, Lord
Why do the animals die?

Men fight battles o'er the sea
The land and in the sky
They thrust and parry, smite and slay
And kill with whom they vie
They sit a-stride their foaming charge
A sword held way up high
Why should it be *they* live, my Lord
And yet the animals die?

Why is it that we take their love
And give them no reply
To bleated braying helplessness
From cooped up pens and sty
Why can't we see the hurt and pain
that lingers in their eye
As death cuts short unspoken words
Why do I have to die
My Lord
Why *do* I have to die?

Thomas Paul Gidman

TO A SHOT BIRD

Do not put your trust in me,
Fallen bird,
Frail, quintessent, throbbing thing,
Brave, absurd.
Light as a skeletal leaf,
Spun in pain.
Through water-melon skies of
Autumn rain
From journeys charted by the
Sun's tall spars,
And silent fantasy in
Fields of stars.
To extinguish a spark so
Small and brief,
In man's scheme of things costs
Little grief.
But as life dissolves in a
Blood-bright ring,
Do the birds of Paradise
Cease to sing?

Wendy Hooper

I WASN'T BORN IN SOMERSET

I wasn't born in Somerset,
I came from London years ago,
So let me tell you of the place,
Which I have come to cherish so.

Rolling hills and fields of green,
Country lanes which twist and turn,
Cottages and pretty churches,
Hedgerows high and banks of fern.

Rivers winding, cattle grazing,
Sunsets red and miles of sky,
Coastal walks and mewing seagulls
On the gentle breezes fly.

I have made so many friends
Here where time keeps gentle pace
And every day I see the smiles
On many a dear and friendly face.

I'm glad I came to Somerset
All those many years ago,
Though I know I'm still a Londoner,
That's something that I can't outgrow.

But now I'm settled, I won't move,
I do not have the need to roam,
Yes, here I'll stay in Somerset
My love is here, this is my home.

Patricia Catling

BIGGY

His face is fat and jolly, and hair springs from his head
In strands of auburn glory. Big shares my lonely bed
At first rejected, lost and sad, a present for my son
Travelling away to Uni pad was really quite good fun.

But back he came, unused, ignored, was not my son's true scene
Others would poke, prod, laugh at him, Biggy the old has been.
Now, coming back into my life, seemingly oh so dear
Better than any man or wife, he lies so snug, so near

Biggy can never answer back, laughs not nor sheds a tear
Big is the quietest thing on earth, yet takes away all fears.
When night time comes he comforts me, just by his being here
Closer than any, yet you know I should not hold him dear.

Softer and warmer than any man, there are no legs or feet
Nor bones to dig or fingers pinch, in bed so snug and sweet
He cannot snore, nor fart or burp, Biggy's so very smart
At keeping still, even turns with me, so really takes his part

In keeping me a happy girl, he and me cannot fight
We lie there dreaming heavenly things, blissful until it's light
How could a human serve me so; when all the shoutings cease
Weary and limp as my rag doll. How can I get some *peace!*

Miserable, groping to small spare room, Big is there all alone
He will not kick or swear, I know, nor even give a moan
Wanting to take up all the space, or wonder if we should
Make love together after all. His life is as of wood.

No puppet there, just a rag doll. No flesh or blood!
You are not real - nor answer back, when I shout loud
'True love I seek, hearts bound forever, and at my death
Place roses on my grave, say 'For eternity I will love her'

Is this an ideal world we seek, meanwhile with hope endeavour
Remember friends both dreamt and real abide in hearts forever

Gwenda Jenkins

HOW?

How do you write a poem
That is bound to win
The biggest competition?
Is wishing such a sin?

I sit down with the paper
Lining pencils in a row,
Drinking coffee by the gallon -
But no words seem to flow.

I joined a local writing course,
'Writing just for you',
The people were quite interesting -
They had this problem too.

I tried a little notebook,
Listing down each thought.
I also tried a holiday,
Then wrote down what I bought.

I don't know if I will achieve
My greatest one desire;
But I've bought a stack of paper,
To write on by the fire.

Heather Nelson

EATING FOR HEALTH

When our innards get fits of the blues
We put bran in the foods that we choose,
In our cornflakes, our cakes, soups and stews.
(But one thing for sure we'll refuse
Is a scheme for polluting our booze.)

If it's roughage we need - we'll be rough,
To make sure that our insides get tough.
Apple peel by the yard we will stuff.
Fruit and bran will fill up our plum duff
Till of roughage we're having enough.

I hope that this verse will not make things worse
But bring cheer to a healthy new diet.
It might seem a bind,
But - Oh well, never mind.
I'm just off myself now to try it.

A Cotter

A POTENTIAL HERO

All you've ever wanted
Is about to come true,
But I stand in the way
Of the dream you must pursue.

The monopoly of loss is mine,
A love that ends before its time;
To watch you go I cannot bear,
To make you stay would not be fair.

Now the time has arrived
I will try to pretend
That you were never my lover,
Only a friend;

But when you are stood there
On the front line
Remember I'm here
If you change your mind.

Kate Ellis

FROM THE HEART

We dance beneath the waning
Moon,
The light upon us sparkles,
By day my eyes hide true intent
behind my darkened glasses,
I try to reach you every night
and take you to different places,
On our travels, you and me
we see the many faces

We see the face of the moon,
We see the face of the night,
We see the face of natural instinct
but we cannot face it's might

We see the face of each
other, the sparkle in our eyes,
By night no need to tell bad
truths as these are worse
than lies

P C Gooding

CHELSEA FLOWER SHOW

Look at me and marvel - tell me, am I not superb?
Where else displayed such glory and surely you have heard
The words of admiration and the worship in the eyes
Of those who see my beauty flaunted bright or in disguise.
My perfume overpowering changes subtly as you pass
To gaze upon my splendour in fresh air or under glass.
If you can find some blemishes within this work of art
Perhaps I'm trying too hard to please and catch your wayward heart.
But rest assured I'll be quite changed when you again appear
To marvel and to gaze once more, same time, same place next year.

Paddy Jupp

DREAMING BY THE SHORE

As I walk along the shore, close to the water's edge, each stride imprints upon the sand and I look behind and watch them slowly fill as a wave washes over them.

It's a cold, crisp December day and the beach is deserted, with only the sound of the waves crashing the shore and the far off cry of a distant gull to interrupt the quietude.

My thoughts turn to the summer when this beach will ring to the sound of children's laughter. The hum of people enjoying the warmth of the sand and the sea amid much splashing and frolicking will create a very different scene.

A wave crashes over my foot and brings me back from reverie. The cry of seagulls now pierces my mind as they hover above the waves, searching for a morsel.

The sea takes on a grey reflection of the sky. Darkness comes early and all the footprints disappear as the sea creeps up the beach,

Val Callicott

JEWEL OF CORNWALL (ST MICHAEL'S MOUNT, MARAZION)

Jewel of the ocean, queen of the tides
Worth our devotion, Neptune's bride,
A light in the storm, a star in the night,
Your regal charms shining so bright.
Like a crown on the waves,
Like a sceptre at sea,
Calling to all men 'Behold and be free!'
Mount of Zion, Rock of St Levan
Jewel of all ages, Mountain of Heaven.

Elaine Pomm

OF BALLOONS AND BUBBLES

It's all a matter of perception,
Or so it seems to me,
Maybe some rogue brain cells deception
Of how things ought to be,
When faced with life's quota of trouble,
Is it bully balloon
Or is it just a bursting bubble,
Hoping to reach the moon?
Sometimes I feel persistent pressure
As the bulging balloon
Tries to smother me for its pleasure
To make me die too soon.
Try as I might to prod it away,
Another bulge appears,
In brash defiance of me to say,
'Don't wipe away your tears,
I'll bother you a little longer,
Until you learn to smile,
As you become stronger and stronger,
Being changed all the while.
Then look good and hard at your trouble,
Till you begin to see
No balloon bully but a bubble,
Bursting to set you free.'

Winifred Rickard

BEECHES IN AUTUMN

Pretty, poised, patient, waiting,
holding golden patterned skirts,
glinting rich with goldcrest glowing
draw-stringed laced by green-finch flirting.

Standing patient, heads held high,
shyly proud, twig fingers holding
secrets glowing, nacarat golden
as long-tailed tits silver whisper.

Leafy processions of pretty skirts,
held so dainty. Wrens fill still air,
tuneful, fluteful, rejoicing joyful
in goldcrest gold and green-finch flirting,

Autumn sodden. Glory fading.
Downpours of leaves drift crestfallen,
Winter is certain. Fingers patient
for skirts of spring-green and goldcrest Autumn.

Thomas Duggan

FORGOTTEN FREEDOM

Footsteps within September days
Voices, sounds changing ways
In the silence that he came
Forever drowning the dying pain.

Locked behind the freedom gate
Trapped among the tempting fate,
Spoken words in the breeze,
Of myself shall not he cease.

Split second forever long
Ended sharply, timing gone
A world of safety of which I stood
Escaping from what I could.

Past the one like never before
In shock, fear and everything more,
Arrival of tenses and those of nerves
Upon the nightmare no-one deserves.

Karen Cook

POPPIES

As the sun breaks through
the early morning mists,
scarlet petals break out
from tight closed buds.
Softly crumpled, they open
to reveal, a black painted middle,
a face upturned
to the warm sun.
What joy, of poppies in the long grass,
their beauty so soon to be gone
with the winds of the coming storm.
Scarlet tears, scattered,
mourning the shortness of life.

Ruby Charlton

TWILIGHT

There is a place called *Twilight,*
Where the *not so perfect* go.
Its misty hills and meadows,
Are cold and deep in snow.

The shadows of lost souls,
They stumble *to and fro.*
The despondence in their hearts,
No mortal man can know.

Their only hope, a glimmer,
A faint and distant glow.
Is the pathway to the heaven,
Where the *good and righteous* go.

D A Hynes

CHANGING TIMES

Standing tall upon the hill
Upon the meadow and in the valley
Ruins now, of a time long past
When their steam driven lifts
Took men to work and home again.

These tall chimneys standing, still
Wooden lintels over door and sill
Still intact they hold in place
The granite stones above them
Some loosened from the mortar grip.

Many a storm has passed them by
Wind and rain and noon-day sun
The freezing cold of a winter's night
The burning sun of a summer's day
Yet still they stand, tall and proud.

Power houses once they were
Lifting tin and copper out
From beneath the fertile land
While high above, cattle grazed
And cereal crops too, were raised.

New landmarks have appeared here now
Large dishes upon Goonhilly downs
Receiving signals from out of space
Large windmills quietly turning
Provide electric for the grid.

A hundred years or so from now
Will they be there and working still
Or will they fall into disrepair
Left to rust and decay there
To show a power of some time past.

Bernard Grose

MOON, METAL AND GLANCE

Cloudy sky so dark yet light,
Moon behind so silver white,
Men at the cliff base still and pale,
Waiting for the lugger's sail.

Voices are whispers excitement is rising,
Thinking of crates soon to be prising,
Will it be silks, jewels or whisky,
Rum, brandy, whatever, it's risky.

Custom's men lurking hoping for sight,
Maybe they'll catch them red handed tonight,
They have the problems, they're only a few,
Just one with experience, the others are new.

Wind is rising, clouds are shifting,
Moon is bright and shows men drifting,
They have seen the glint of metal,
Custom's men know this is fatal,

Now the night is growing quieter,
Men are leaving, night is brighter,
Custom's men have lost a chance,
Because of moon, metal and glance.

J Guy

CROSSROADS

I feel the sunshine on my back
Scorching heat burning my skin
Perishing flowers look so sad
Just like my faith they're dying

The ground below is too hot to walk on
Dusty roads, dried up and cracking
Clear skies, no rain today
Just like my religion it's lacking

I come across the sea of life
A wave of confusion drags me under
I struggle hard and learn to fight
Triumph over my indecision

D J Smith

DRUGS POEM

I'm OK, another day, I'll stop tomorrow, another J, to drown my sorrow.
Sorrow of a lost life, sorrow of a lost soul, living life without a goal.
Self denial, dishonesty, hypocritical preachings not for me.
In the trap, bars in my face, my face no more,
the sorrow in my eyes, another J, drown those feelings raw.
Thump in the back, no it's my mate, that ain't working, drugged on slate.
Got any gear, got any draw, got any puff mate, got any more,
more than last time, another drink, another glass of wine,
got any Billy, Billy you ain't silly,
I ain't hooked, I'm fine, I'll stop tomorrow, got any trips, to drown my sorrow.
Life fading in a blur of yesterdays, got any Charlie, lay me on some,
I'll pay you, I'll pay you, I'll find ways,
to support my habit, trying to quit life, escape with false pleasure,
ecstasy in heaven, got any more, increase my measure, you know the score.
Another friend gone, what's it worth, what are we here for mother earth.
Three fifty wrap, lay me on some smack, injecting, can't do any harm,
where's it grown? Death farm?
The dying weed, as I smoke I bleed, bleeding life from my vein,
                                                             nothings the same.
Rave, rave, rave, last week I done pot, whack, smack, crack, backy, Billy,
aren't you silly,
Bill how've you been, long time no see, you've changed, you look mean,
what have you been up to, nothing much, nothing much, stoned again,
missed it, pissed it, fuck it, up my life, up my arm, up my lung, up my nose,
yeah it shows, see ya later Bill, take care friend.

Kali Heffernan

THE YAWNING BEAR

The lands are covered with an array of heathered beauty,
Goonhilly Culdrose, the beauty of St Kevern, nature predominantly
showing beauty among the suffocation of man, the heath land
and heathered beauty kissed by summer sun, serpentine stone this
land of the yawning bear, brightened with love by summer daylight
petals of beauty sing delight, a touch of sweetness upon your
hand whispered beauty upon the land, so many wonders to see,
through wooded valley to Mullion, thatched cottages, whisper
stories of smugglers' mystic times, heathers lay as silken cloth.
Lizzard Point heathland and heathered beauty kissed by summer
sun, serpentine stone, this land of the yawning bear, how your
beauty touches me, as child your beauty light shines.

The touch of beauty upon the summer sea, lift upon the
breeze, when summer light will touch the trees, and all
nature shows so true of the love held sweetly for you,
the light of the day so bright sweet children at peace at rest
mafter play sweet passions of love so true, sweetly shine for
you, whispers the touch the yawning bear, sweet passions.

N J Steel

FEELINGS

How can I explain my feelings for you?
They live in the mind and words simply won't do.
I tried it with actions but mostly they're wrong
And you won't find them echo in the words of a song.

To say that I love you isn't telling it all.
The words, sincere as they are, sound far too cold.
I want you, I need you: don't help clarify.
Simply where you are, so too am I.

Dee Kimber

STARTERS BOOM

Rippled water and blackened
sky,
A sudden squall approaching,
Watch the Burgee the set of
the sails,
The sudden heel as the canvas
Fills and we bow before the
wind.
The exhilaration of moving fast
Leaning back to improve the
trim
A salty taste upon our lips
The pleasures, now the race
is on.

Eric Drake

GIFTS OF AUTUMN

Autumn leaves are falling
They have turned a burnished gold,
What splendour in the countryside
As the months of the year unfold.

Fruits of autumn ripe to pick
Delicious treats in store.
Beautiful wild flowers still to be found
On earth's wild and wonderful floor.

It is nature's store of riches
I believe it was nature's plan.
To share these gifts with everyone
These are God's gifts to man.

Carol Alway

THE EMBRACE

With death there is finality,
With the last embrace you have to live without,
Yet there is a continuance of life, of love,
In the false finale there is no satisfaction of ultimate
                                  indisputable loss
The potential lies in the arms unleashed, in the heart burning
The possibility is within reach, but the sun is setting
And love is lost in the dark.
The soul can only dance desperately amongst the fading rays
Raking and trawling the memories to feed the last few hours
There will be no return if the horizon swallows the light
Sweeping existence into blackness with the curve of its arm
So velvet and tender it could only be the last.
Time will have no meaning, the seconds breathing backwards into hours.
If there had been knowledge would that last embrace have been hysterical?
Would the sun have swollen and burst, tears of liquid gold flooding the land?
Could the agony have been washed away in the cries of a heated soul?

Kate Tilley (17)

LEARNED AND LEARNER

The children know
All about you
And they know what they were talking about too
But were they happy?
You want your good looks
They want the books
When they want your attention you are snappy!
Little time to burn
Not right to preach
They want to learn
So teach!

Clifford J D Hart

BOSNIA? OR ANYWHERE

Try as I might, I just can't understand,
How killing a child for the sake of some land,
Is looked on as some kind of God given right,
To the soldier who's chosen to take up the fight.

A town is surrounded, there's an order to fire,
With every explosion, the death toll grows higher,
A young child lies dying in a street far below,
The invisible target of a too distant foe,
Poor soldier, they say, he wasn't to know,
That this one cowardly act, could have done so much harm,
But does he look on, with a sense of alarm?
No, he's a pro. and is trained to stay calm.

Meanwhile, a young mother seeks out her child's hand,
But that child has died. . .
For the sake of some land,

S R Lucie

PEACE

The papers have been signed
the fighting left behind
We make a vow to kill and fight no more.
We call each other friend
we are glad it's at an end
but do not step in the blood upon the floor.
For it's the blood of everyone
who died from bomb or gun
who died for a cause they paid dearly for.
If death to them came swift
it is only nature's gift
for everyone who found their peace in war.

John Mostyn-Bond

ELECTIVE MUTE

Somewhere distant a bell sounded
Muffled by clouds it went unheeded
And I proceeded
Full of hope.

A Klaxon warned - false start!
Determined and focused with face to the wind
I shifted gear
Not looking behind.

A siren wailed ill-omen
Head down, unfettered
I blundered on
Regardless of other's laces undone.

A hand tugged at my sleeve
Insistent that I listen
Shoving fear inside my back-pack
I shrugged loose
And hummed
A tune of defiance and derision.

'Am I going too fast for you?' He said
As he loaded up my red leather chair
With the rest of my world in the back of the van
And headed for 'Home'.

The bell rang out, the klaxon warned
The siren wailed, the voice implored
The hand tugged at my vocal chords
Scooped out
Stricken
I turned
And said. . .
Nothing.

Rosie Cornish

EARTH MOTHER

Mother
I wait for you in oceans
tide
washes my thoughts
back and forward

Sky
shifts above me
stars
touch the dark infinity
find me before I am lost

I search
for dainty shells to
decorate
my secret hideaway
I listen for your voice

Mother
your song caresses me
with
gentleness, waves lap at
my feet. I am yours, take me

I laugh
when you touch me.
Sand
is white now, I write your
name and it vanishes as tide

pulls words out.
Mother
I wait for you to touch my heart
and hold me forever

Teresa Webster

NEVER WORSE OFF

Like marble statue, I took my stance
And over cliff top edge did glance
Above my head the lightning flashed
Beneath my feet the ocean crashed
On rocky top where seagulls dare
Unmoved by storm I stand and stare.

For here there lies beauty
Though the sky's dark as night,
What were calm lazy waves
Take on a new might.
My clothing does little
To keep out the cold
As I spot on the beach
A man, twisted and old.
Rain, hail or shine
He's always at hand
To collect the wet driftwood
That lies on the sand
A lonely old soul
Now without wife
Collects wood for the fire
That keeps him alive
As the winds they grow colder
I still stand alone
The forgotten war hero
Scrambles off home
The old medal ribbon still pinned to his side
I've lost my love and he's lost his pride.

R Morris

SUNDAY

Sunday sat in the window
Oh what a place to sit
He watched the birds in the hedgerow
Sparrows, blackbirds and bluetits
He wondered in anticipation
Just how good they would taste
So, down he jumped from the window
And out the back door in great haste

He crept along the pavement
Until he reached the bend
He licked his lips with excitement
His body twitched from end to end
He flicked his tail quite madly
The blackbird he could see
You'll do me just right thought Sunday
You will make a lovely tea

The birds they sat there singing
Oblivious to what was about
Sunday was ready to spring
When he heard his mistress shout
What are you doing Sunday
You know you don't catch birds
You are supposed to be a mouser
But that would be absurd

Sunday jumped back up in the window
But he did not wish to sit
To watch the birds in the hedgerow
Sparrows, blackbirds and bluetits
Instead he lay in the window
Happy to sleep and dream
Of fish, meat and biscuits
And possibly some cream

Rita Parfitt

SONG OF A WEST COUNTRY WOMAN

Oh, I envy the confident women of Surrey and Berks and Bucks and Kent -
The self-possessed classes with arrogant arses and busts which declare their
                                                              intent.
They have no need for guile, supercilious smile or sneer to express their
                                                              disdain;
It's their posture and gait and their hauteur I hate, and their poise which
                                                           I never attain.

Yes, I envy the confident women of Kent and Surrey and Berks and Bucks
Whose men are so dumb that they meekly succumb to the lure of
                                                           coiffure de luxe.
The style of their skirts and the shape of their shirts and the cut of their
                                                            coats betoken
Pure condescension with no apprehension towards less prosperous folk.

How I envy the confident women of Bucks and Kent and Surrey and Berks!
They command when they speak, the attention they seek - it's announcements
                                                         they make, not remarks.
Their delivery crisp, without trace of a lisp, represents the executive norm;
Their selection of phrase, their choice of clichés confirms managerial form.

God! I envy the confident women of Berks and Bucks and Kent and Surrey.
They entertain grandly, they blaspheme blandly and never make love
                                                            in a hurry.
With effortless ease they insist on their fees - status, respect and esteem.
Their coolness in crisis, their freedom from vice is acknowledged by all
                                                           as supreme.

I'm impure, insecure and I'm shaped like a skewer and talk like a
                                                           country bore
And I'm coarse and I'm hoarse and I'm full of remorse and I dress like
                                                        a camel - what's more,
When I go up to bed and I wait there for Fred, he's no sooner come
                                                          than he's went.
Which would never occur to him or to her in Surrey, Berks, Bucks or Kent.

Anne Pethereck

LUNDY FOLK

It was a glorious summer's day
A sunny day in June;
The sun had ruled the golden hours -
At night it was the moon.
'Twas on a simple Channel ship.
Balmoral was her name;
We sailed the Bristol Channel
And to Lundy Island came.
There she stood, erect and proud,
Defiant as the Law -
As we stepped into the little boats
And gently came ashore.
Assisted by the Lundy folk -
Ashore without a fuss,
Then someone in the boat remarked,
'They look the same as us . . . '

Jimmie Cross

THE GOSSAMER HOUR

The tall green silhouettes
Of the many wintered trees
Grouped around the tumbling stream
Which falls beneath their knees.
The ever moving yet still pond
Is rippled with droplets of rain.
From the branches is hung
Morning's finest jewel
Delicate strings of Gossamer
Fit for a queen's neck
But crowning nature's King.

Annabelle Ough

MID-WEEK BREAK

It wasn't my idea to go in the mini.
It wasn't my idea to take the hamper.
My only idea was to take the snake
But all you said was, 'Why?

> Why do you want to take the snake?
> This is our mid-week break
> Our one chance to view
> The motorway's hues.'

It was not my idea to take the A10.
It was not my idea to take the kids.
I innocently suggested the snake
And you said 'Why? Why? Why?

> Why do you want to take the snake?
> This is our mid-week break -
> Our one chance to view
> The motorway's hues.'

And I said to my darling wife, 'Well dearest,
If we are lucky it might eat the hamper,
It might eat the mini, A10 and kids,
And of course you dearest.'

Damon Naile

A DARTMOOR NONSENSE

I went awalking with my dog
Through miles; and miles; and miles of bog.
We thought we'd try a little higher,
But ended up in Foxtor Mire.

You'll want to hear the aftermath,
Which simply was - a nice warm bath.

Peter Lee

THE BILLIARD ROOM HAS GONE

The high backed chairs remain, pink plush,
Empty they stand to wait another day.
Indented cushions lie with shawls forgotten,
Strewn papers, frames, and one neglected stick.
The living dead are safely put to bed,
Odour, yet faint, remains of outlived souls,
In the one-time billiard room.

On such a summer's night,
Male bellicose laughter mingled
With heavy Havana'd air,
The rich at play, their women set aside.
Clash of cue and ball, and ribaldry,
Swirled brandy coloured in the glass.

But now the vacant room has echoes
Of shuffling day, of mind's bewilderment,
Fluttering fingers, and forgotten shoes,
Splintered memories in pale eyes.
From Georgian corniced walls,
Pampered portraits stand immune
To relicts, who asked not this.

Gracious house, built with such art and style,
How see you now the world? Your lawns
Are bare and bleak, no gaiety of balls,
No silken hems to trail the noble stairs.
A delicate hand, lightly upon the rail,
Is yellow parchment, and crab-veined.

Carol Exten-Wright

GRANDMA

Friend, lover, mistress, wife!
All these you've been to me.
The years have treated you kindly
Which is plain for all to see.
Now life has sent another role
One meant for only you!
'Grandma' is the name for it,
I know you'll see it through.
Cuddles, kisses, lots of love
All these you can give,
To our little grandchildren
For as long as you shall live.
But! Save a few for Grampa
As time goes swiftly by,
He also loves his *Grandma*
You're the apple of his eye!
And as we both get older
I know that you won't mind,
If we share the role together
Two hearts, two souls, one mind.

R Ninnis

THOUGHT

Within the depths of sleep,
There lies an energy,
To conquer and abide by its ruler.
Control is within reach,
Strike at will,
To entice such power,
All be at your knees.
Withering under control.

Chichieun Wong

THE PASSING OF PUSS!

Those little legs still very weak,
That so rich coat of fluffy fur,
That whiskered face which did love seek,
That almost inaudible purr.
He would thrust forth in morning joy
His head erect his tail held high
And like a Red Indian boy:
He'd climb a tree up to the sky.
But 'twas not always just the sky.
Sometimes the curtains would be his that day:
He'd run, he'd tear, pretend to die,
Just like his brothers did at play.
Now chair legs he'd go for,
Complete from top to toes.
And dive right through the open door
Attacking all such foes.
Then after evening's pleasures
The prowling puss came back in joy;
Depositing his treasures:
A cotton reel or little toy,
My little pussy comes to bed
His world of enemies disband,
And triumphant lies his head
In the palm of my hand.
My little curious ball of play
When you sallied out to fight
My heart's grieved since that fated day
When you came not home that night
Cursed be that motor car -
It laid you low, so fast from far.

G Halfpenny

GRANF

The ripe old age of ninety-two
He's always finding things to do,
Had his ups and downs I know,
Look at his face it doesn't show.

He's so busy all the while
Chirpy words and knowing smile
Nothing really gets him down
You hardly ever see a frown.

When he throws up that skittle ball
Ten to one the pins will fall.
It's been his life, he's still quite keen
Started playing when just sixteen.

Good gardener he's always been
With his produce often seen,
Fruit and veg. and flowers as well
His sweet peas with lovely smell.

Life was hard in his younger days
But sounds quite good in many ways.
Things he got up to in days of old
Some funny stories I've been told.

So times were hard but I will bet
With Fred there's nothing he'll regret.
He's sailed right through the changing tide
Everything taken in his stride.

Margaret Whitehead

THE OLD LADY

How long has she sat in that green, upright chair,
In the corner of the room?
The chair so straight and tall,
She so frail and bent.
Last week I came.
Last year I came.
She sits there still.

When I look at her what do I see?
An old, sad lady - her days now gone.
The world moves on,
She's left behind.
Needing feeding, washing, changing.
She sits there still.

Heads four generations of her kin,
For whom she once washed and cooked.
Does she remember being young?
Now alone,
She cannot say,
What she would change.
She sits there still.

And yet inside her worn out shell,
Perhaps her mind is clear and strong.
Could it be she looks at me,
Rushing by,
No time to spare,
And thanks God that
She sits there still?

Sally Wyatt

TORMENT

Intent on destroying,
My heart and my soul,
Thy rip me to pieces
Creating this hole,
Yank at my feelings,
Then load me with guilt.
Expect me to be there
But maybe I won't.

You sang for your master
Then made me your slave,
For him you chase after,
While I'm left to crave,
Devoid of emotion,
When we are alone,
Expect me to be there,
But then who knows.

You dance when he asks,
Then shout when I cry,
Enter his room,
While alone I lie,
Your breathing increases
My last breath I breathe
You expected,
Far too much from me.

Andrew Carter

I LOVE YOU

A gardener's work is never done,
He's always on the go,
Digging this and planting that
With spade and fork and hoe.

He's out all day no matter what
I don't know where he's gone,
He's in the greenhouse down the path
With his seedlings - potting on.

With wellies on and tools to hand,
He patiently sows his seeds,
We don't run short of veggies,
He supplies our daily needs.

Sometimes he'll curse and shout out loud,
When he finds out that he's bleeding,
So I get the box to clean him up,
But he's gone to do the weeding.

The evening's here, it's getting dark,
It's time to think of sleep,
But there he is just dozing off,
Beside the compost heap.

I wake him up and bring him in,
And make sure that he's fed,
He says 'I love you garden,'
As I tuck him up in bed.

V Stock

THIS LIFE OF EXTREMES

Oh for the peace and the joy of the free.
Birds in the air, migrating so free,
The fish in the sea, no barriers to fear,
The plants in the river
The lakes and the streams,
The clouds in the sky,
The waves on the sea,
The frost in the air
The snow on the peaks,
The trees and the fields,
Oh what a gift, for you and for me,
Air and the sunshine, the freedom to breathe,
Thunder and lightning, flashing so free,
Volcanic action, with orange gold streams,
Making fresh islands come out of the sea,
I think and I wonder,
This life of extremes,
I look in amazement,
I'm so glad I can see,
And to hear the birds singing,
The roar of the sea,
The peace of the meadows,
The falling of leaves,
The cry of the new born
In this land that is free.
We curse it, criticise it,
Condemn it if needs,
But we'll fight to the last,
For our dear country.

Norrie Hill

THE CANALS OF ENGLAND

In days gone by, when the pace of life
Was slower than today.
The canals of England seemed to be
A cost effective way
Of moving freight from here to there
By boat or horse drawn barge.
People realised the need
For the network to enlarge.
To get by sea from north to south
Of England's south west arm
Was treacherous, to say the least.
Ships often came to harm.
Plans were made for a watery road
To be built across the land.
Excitement at the prospect
One can understand.
But the best laid plans of man can fall
In to hasty disrepute,
But the wisdom of the foresight
No-one can dispute,
In modern times these old canals
Are busy once again.
Restored to former glory
Tradition is maintained.
Now leisure has replaced the freight.
Engines oust the horse.
The canals of England live again
For pleasure now, of course.

Alan Potter

THE SEASONS

Daffodils dancing in the breeze
Birds singing in the trees
New born lambs what joy they bring
They all are celebrating spring.

Children paddling in the sea
Oh how carefree they can be
Mums and dads in deck-chairs laze
Just the thing for summer days.

Leaves floating to the ground with ease
Encouraged by the gentle breeze
Squirrels hunting for nuts to store
Autumn has arrived once more.

Shorter days and longer nights
Snowflakes falling and Christmas lights
Robins perching on the sill
Sheltering from the winter chill.

J Hawkins

INSPIRATION

A grey storm cloud that drifts away.
A green moor in the light of the day.
A Guernsey cow that chews the cud.
A scraggy dog that trails through the mud.
A mirror that's too foggy to look in.
A cat that is searching through a bin.
All these and more, they give inspiration,
To a poet or artist or writer who breeds them,
Into a masterpiece created by mind,
For a reader or looker or listener to find.

Laura David

FLOWERS OF THE FIELD

Dead men now lie where flowers once swayed,
Face down in the filth - the price has been paid,
Where green grass was lush and scent flowed on the breeze,
Men now with rifles are on hands and knees.

With a mission to kill and a target in sight,
What is the point? It just doesn't seem right,
That innocent men should be killed in this way,
While the families of fighters suffer day after day.

Another day is passing with nothing really won,
The terrors of the day disappear with the evening sun,
Armies from all countries fight with opposing powers,
But now memories of death have merged together with the flowers

So when the fighting and the gunfire all have died away,
And grass shoots through muddy earth and the flowers begin to sway,
And barbed wire barricades have been taken down,
For all humans to roam, white, yellow or brown,
and the warfields looked as they looked before,
But scars still remain the hearts of those who fought in this pointless war.

What is a medal or what is a plaque?
What's your name worth engraved in stone,
If you're never coming back

Miranda Hodder

THE TINY SEED OF LOVE

The tiny seed of love,
You women of poverty, rich or poor
If you're with child and don't know what to do,
Turn to our dear Lord for He loves you

Do not think of yourself
        Think of your unborn child
Do not let self-pity destroy your pride.

Do not have an abortion if need not be,
        So let your child come into
        This world - like you and me.

Remember Our Blessed Lady Mary
        Was humble and poor
She gave Jesus his birth within a stable door
So let your child have life - do not destroy
        For you'll never know if it's a girl or a boy.

Please remember your children are
        the children of tomorrow.
Your children are a special gift
        the greatest gift of love.

Please open up your hearts
        and think of that tiny seed
That was planted with love
        from the very start.

Lucille Hope

MARINE DRIVE

On land I look to windows
Where glass panes transpose
The wet world of wind blown wild
And graving gone from time
By striving in a hurling space.
Unfurled are breaths of calling
Brave with a banner's shout
Into the sad storm's eye
That will not blink but blinding
Salt the deep sprays that spangle
The throbbing hours of morning.
Ah! The ache of soughing air!
Take on no love but hunger cruelly
For its despair: demeaned and losing
There unsatisfied of surfeits -
There is wind too much and too much
Scud and clouds and wetness
Flushed in a threshing universe
Of wailing water lashed beneath
A gale's spread dome of strato-nimbus
Dense and thrawn and fraught
With comfort for a bleak haven:
No feeling fear, lack fear
That feeds high shrieking harmonies
Plucked from tautened wires which bend
A soul's howling: howling and yearning
For a warming love-knot cold a-blessing.
Rock me good night not falsely home
Made fairly dwelling.

Leonard Fifield

SNOW IN CORNWALL

It is so very still -
The hills lie close,
Amazed to see the snow
And ancient pastures tell
Of those rare springs
When winter lagged behind
As it does now.

The cottage roofs are white
Preening themselves
In new-found innocence;
Only the church tower,
Being vertical,
Resists the soft embrace,
Thinking of sterner things.

If it should freeze tonight
My polyanthus
Will bow their heads in shame
To think their trustfulness
Was so misplaced
And my old bones
Will bitterly complain
Alas, for winter
Has come back again.

Francis Middleditch

CAESAR - THE CAT

Sleek, arrogant, mysterious
A distant presence
Always elusive
Fur hardly ruffled,
Your gaze, confident and settled.

With unhurried movement
Measured, cautious, deft
Your tread is silent
On the faded cobble stones
Foreboding, chills my bones.

You squint, wink, blink
Finally staring, peering, preparing
Slowly you arch your back
Your unsuspecting prey you track
Ready to attack.

Sleek, elegant, determined
With shadowy, movement skilled
Suddenly, poised to pounce
Ruthless, without remorse
Instinctively, you've killed.

Anne Cleife

OCTOBER

The brittle hems of autumn leaves
Scratching at my window pane
Like sickle claws of frantic birds
Desperate to escape the icy rain . . .

Diana Stannus

THE SPIRIT OF PLACE

The Spirit of Place is nowhere now
Travelling man is dead
Those longing hills, that tranquil spot
Have died inside his head.
No more quick cities glistening white
Beneath the mid-day sun,
No more received Earth's sights and sounds
In human cranium.
Green forests, streams and rocky places
Speak through a silenced ear
The fleshy brain has long since gone
Eyes' visions disappeared.
Such tracks and pathways firmly led
Across cerebral bands
A bony void inherits now
Life's lie of magic lands.
Man roams no more across the globe
The Spirit of Place is gone
The homely plane has since dissolved -
Is there another one?

Grenville Gilbert

NEW AGE

When kindred spirits unite as one
and night turns into day
We'll walk together hand in hand
each step along the way
Joy and love and tranquil minds
will ease the pain and sorrow
Staunch our mothers bleeding heart
create a new tomorrow.

Chris Glover

DARTMOOR, THE MYSTIQUE

Dartmoor. This mystic land for one thousand years or more.
If only these rocks could talk, they have much more in store,
of the people and their families that once roamed these lands,
Which are now so barren, that the elements have the upper hand.
The hot steamy sun to start you off in the seasonal swelter.
Changes to the Arctic cold in winter, with no apparent shelter.

Six rivers guard these majestic rocks of many ages.
They cascade downwards into valleys of rare places.
Through acres of woodland, oak and birch.
Creating miles of nature trails, which you are allowed to search.
The beauty of Dartmoor is conserved for all to see.
The tranquillity of life moves like the workings of a bee.

Further in the moor, the landscape changes its wondrous texture,
from monstrous Tors to rolling lanes of green pasture.
Ponies roam wild and free, through this mystic, ageless land.
The sheep take no notice, wandering at will. It wasn't planned.
Go to the top of a Tor, where the clouds are above your head,
and survey this barren land with its wondrous dead.

The picturesque villages with their customs dotted there,
create a timeless era, with splendour and fayre.
Once more let's walk through the graveyards of time,
these people, our heritage, lay there so benign.
When I grow old and life offers no care,
I wish to come back to Dartmoor, I surely belong there.

Edward A Walker

SPRINGTIME IN DEVON

Spring has always been my favourite time of year,
and now living in Devon it has become quite clear.
How it has earned the name of glorious Devon,
For to me it is like a little piece of Heaven.
First appear the snowdrops who seem to be telling you,
Nature is wonderful and beginning anew.
Then appear the primroses, all along the banks,
Making us feel happy, and so full of thanks.
Then the daffodils in various shades of yellow,
Gladden our hearts, so that we feel quite mellow.
They seem to be everywhere, also down by the river,
We really must be grateful to the Lord our giver.

Now it soon will be bluebell time again,
Why, we could all sing a happy refrain,
For there will be many carpets of blue,
Giving our countryside a wonderful hue.
Birds everywhere are feathering their nest,
And there is very little time for rest.
As spring is the time for renewal of life,
It helps to free us of toll and of strife,
Oh glorious Devon, I do love you so,
I hope to remain here and never go.
Everywhere has its great places of beauty,
But I feel that I just must make it my duty,
To sing the praises of my little heaven,
Here on earth, and it is called Devon.

Carol Diane Milne

THE SPOTTED FLY CATCHER

Silent in flight,
soon out of sight.
Whisking and whirling,
Twisting and twirling.
They dart to and fro,
Which way did they go?
Sharp beaks a-snapping
Thus insects entrapping.
One minute there,
The next minute - where?
This way and that,
A bird acrobat.

The moss nests are lined
with cobwebs entwined.
Flies are the food
They catch for their brood.

Unobtrusive,
Elusive,
Their dancing
Entrancing.

Long will I remember
This May to September -
The fly-catcher's visit
Quiet trust their requisite.
What a welcome waits here
When they come back next year.

Phyl Williams

UNTITLED

The course of true love
doesn't run
smoothly in my back yard it travels
rough
through vegetable patches (nibbling away
at the parsnips) across the crazy paving
and around
the beanpoles strolling past the rockery
speeding
up the garden path straight through
the formal beds skipping
the stepping stones carefully planned
kicking havoc amongst the gooseberries
leaving molehills the size of mountains on the lawn
slime-trails and
discarded cherry stones
half-eaten lettuce-hearts under the rose bush.
Then limps with a thorny paw
and rests on the fence
for a while.
Watching, mischief in mind,
the beleaguered gardener.

Nur-Viktoria Frings

POWERHOUSES OF THE PAST

I sought them out beside the sea,
Perched upon cliff edge perilously,
Ancient monsters from an ancient past
Their granite fortresses were the last

And there they stood as I mounted the hill
Great powerhouses of granite and dill,
With heather growing from beneath the stones;
A giant's body, no flesh but bones

Like sunken eyes scattered around,
Their empty sockets stared up from the ground
And whispering echoes made by the wind,
Chilled the heart of the traveller kind

Tall, granite monuments to power,
To sweat and blood shed by the hour;
In darkest depths it was a sin
How power exploited men for tin.

Roberta Gilman-Grey

CORNWALL

How I love the place where I live
This county of Cornwall has so much to give
Soft golden sands, the sun on my face
Waves that rush in, like frothy white lace

High on the moors the gorse and the heather
Bow down their heads, to all kinds of weather
A patchwork of colour, purple and gold
What a sight to see, a joy to behold

Whitewashed cottages lie in a hollow
A winding road invites you to follow
Flowers glisten in the morning dew
Enhancing this enchanting view

Wherever I travel in this big wide world
Whatever treasures before me unfold
From the Highlands of Scotland to Hadrian's wall
My heart is still captured by lovely Cornwall.

Christine Willis

PLYMOUTH - RESURGAM

You remember the year - 1939
11 o'clock in the morning, that was the time.

But on that cold September day
to the people of Plymouth, war felt far away.

It wasn't long before it came to your door
in a way you had never known before.

Gas masks were issued to one and all
from the eldest down to the very small.

Blackout restrictions were soon made law
all you heard was, 'put out that light' and 'shut that door!'

Anderson shelters became your home
when a bomber's moon 'cross the sky would roam.

Yes, the bombs they fell on many a night,
your homes all gone in the morning light.

Coming up from the shelter with blankets and flask
you wondered how much longer it could last.

But life went on, it didn't stop,
sometimes you went to the Sixpenny Hop.

Dancing the waltz, the quickstep too
with soldiers, airmen and the boys in blue.

Some of you went from the bombing each night,
out on the moors till the morning light.

Then, singing in the streets, bells ringing loud and clear
A sound you thought you would never hear.

Blackouts came down - oh what a treat
letting the lights shine out in the streets.

Flags and bunting, red, white and blue.
People of Plymouth, you had won through!

A new Plymouth, rebuilt, a young generation to see
and it's thanks to your courage that they are all free.

Alice Tall

FOSTER MOTHER

When they needed love you were there
Without hesitation, just a silent prayer
They needed a home, you didn't flinch
Willingly made room where there wasn't an inch!
When they needed care you were tired and ill
You gave your all till they'd had their fill.
When they needed comfort you dried their tears
Just as you had for others over the years
And though you were poor and hadn't enough
You never let on or made it seem tough
There must have been times you felt so alone
With no-one to turn to with grief of your own
A time in your life when you wished he was there
Your loved one was gone and you felt such despair
Yet you took these two babies into your heart
Set aside your pain and played your part
In years to come they will look behind
And remember the times you were good and kind
When they're firmly set along life's path
And you've taught them to live and love and laugh
Don't worry then that you don't break even
The love you are giving is noted in heaven
There's someone who's watching your work my friend
Who'll be there and waiting for you at the end.

Roberta Bell

BULLYING!

I hate his guts,
I with that he were dead.
I shouldn't have these nasty thoughts,
Racing through my head.

But he gives me reasons to have them,
To hate him so very much.
Making me live in fear
With his less than tender touch.

He's at the school gates
Waiting for me to pass
I try to ignore him
But how much longer can I last?

First comes the name calling,
Names like cripple and spas.
I try to limp quickly past him,
But he is far too fast.

Next comes the destruction
Of all of my personal things,
He snatches my bag away from me
Then he notices my ring.

He bends my hand behind my back
And tugs off the ring.
He says he sell it for a quid or two
And warns me not to scream.

Lisa Tonkin

SIX SWANS; ONE SMALL GIRL AND A CAMERA

Three swans
Two white, one black,
Bobbing with pride,
In line ahead:
Breasting the sunlit waters
Of the broad River Taw,
By Barnstaple.

Three others, white and gliding
Sideways pass them.
As soldiers pass
A military saluting base:
All dipping yellow beaks,
Obsequiously.

One little girl,
With her first camera
Assuming proudly grown-up stance:
She shoots,
(Her mother hovering, protectively,
Nearby).
The shutter pressed
The two, relaxed, move on . . .

Leaving the glistening ripples
Of the Taw flowing on, endlessly,
Towards Bideford and Estuary,
Dissolving, merging soundlessly,
Into the vast bosom
Of restless seas
Beyond.

Richard Flemington

OLD AGE

Sitting here in my high back chair
Reliant on others for my care.

My eyes are bad and I cannot see
The faces of the people who tend to me.

I cannot hear what people say
The whole of me is in decay.

My legs are swollen and my feet are sore
It's a terrible effort to walk to the door.

Days are long and go so slow
I cast my mind back long ago.

I used to knit and read for hours
Enjoy my garden and grow lovely flowers.

Why have I lived to be so old
With emotions numb and hands so cold?

Every single night I pray
I do not live another day.

V Murton

THE CHILD THAT NEVER WAS

I weep for the child that never was,
the child yet to be.TConceived only inside my head,
A pretty girl is she.

I grieve for the dresses she'll never wear,
The satins bows and lace.
I'll never stroke the silken hair
That frames her sweet little face.

I feel as though I've really lost her,
Had her, and let her go.
But the only place she ever lived
Was deep inside my soul.

I wanted to be able to see myself
Gently mirrored in she.
I wanted her to see herself
Gently mirrored in me.

There were times I thought I'd never feel,
As someone who was whole.
But the only way to feel complete
Is to learn to let her go.

Anne Harper

ODE TO THE BLACKDOWNS

Would that I could soar like the circling hawk,
Flying free, to view fully your grace.
Your patient serenity captures mine eye,
Your weathered but beautiful face.
Majestic your oaks, and beeches cascading,
Still graceful, tho' gnarled with ageing,
Forming your woodlands, where timid deer browse
For the herbage on which they will feast.
On your verdant green fields graze safely the sheep,
We know there's no panther-like beast.
But we must fight man's greed and lust for more speed,
More highways we surely don't need?
To mar your wild splendour is so great a crime;
To be lost to our children, lost for all time.
We'll protect it with all the love we can give
This wonderful land where we've chosen to live.

Brenda Eyles

THE RIVER

High in the hills, in a cleft in the ground,
Bubbling and gurgling and swirling around.
The birth of a river, here but a stream
Springs from the darkness of caverns unseen.
It forms into puddles which slowly get wider
Then join up together - a long, liquid, finger
It covers the ground with a movement so gentle
Showing no sign of its later potential.
It slips between tussocks and goes on its way
Glinting and sparkling in warm light of day,
It builds up in strength as it covers the hollows.
Then sobs over gravel as if full of sorrows.
It tinkles and twinkles, murmuring softly
With toad and with water rat gambolling gently.
It gets quite assertive round bottoms of hedgerow
Then wanders more slowly 'cross moorland and meadow
As it drops down in height from the hills to the plains
It widens and deepens with successive rains.
As it pours down the valleys its voice changes tone
Getting deeper, more roaring and less of a moan.
It's strength is immense as it first sights the sea,
Then it's harnessed by man to make 'tricity.
They build up great dams as high as a steeple
To hold back the flood for the good of the people.
They pipe it and pump it, to many a place,
To factories and houses and some just to waste,
Then when, in its power, it spills over the top
It falls with a speed which nothing can stop
And continues its journey, down to the sea,
Leaving its blessings, for you and for me.

Paul Cox

TEMPLE TO THE SEA

We stand together, yet far apart,
With destiny upon the night;
Nature, my mother, in my heart like the moon
And the stars all around us;
And the melting, the surging, the quiet sound of the sea
Crashes in the loneliness.
Naked in her power
Her fearsome beauty is revealed
When she slips her tidal cloak;
Silhouetted in time
The unforgiving arms pierce the sky,
Could we but reach beyond
Beyond these walls of granite, walls of grief,
This silent coast, temple to the sea.
While I gaze into the blue
For one moment more, I long to reflect,
But the ghost of some conscience
Echoes like a dream,
Like a shadow in my footsteps
Returning to claim some unwritten debt.
Age on age I have watched
Pass by like the night in fitful slumber;
Then, even as I sigh in the wake of Nature's way,
I will rise and fall upon these shores
Like the moon and the sun before me,
And shine like a hand
Holding the mirror of time
Over this silent coast,
This temple to the sea.

Laura Eves

MAYA

A see through veil hides nature's show
        Displayed before us to be seen
But how to look we rarely know.

The diamond glints of fast stream flow,
        The dappled trout's protective screen.
A see through veil hides nature's show.

Kingfishers dive in currents tow
        Iridescent in blue and green.
But how to look we rarely know.

Hedgerows with firefly calls aglow,
        Shelter for prey to feed and preen.
A see-through veil hides nature's show.

The fleeting shadows as zephyrs blow,
        Shading corn in pastoral scene.
But how to look we rarely know.

Evening flights of curlew and crow,
        Open fields to furrow and glean.
A see-through veil hides nature's show,
        But how to look we rarely know.

Ray Dite

A ROOM WITH A VIEW

A tiny world that I have lived in
a World that's ten feet small
a World of broken dreams
a World I take no more

There's a view outside my window
of a World that feels so small
a view of rows of houses
and endless garden walls

If I stretch I can see the water
through a gap between the walls
or the man who stands right opposite
like a mirror on the wall

From this room I've felt so lonely
I've tried to plan it all
which road that I should take now
to break down these four walls

But this room, it's not a giving
the walls stand firm and tall
the only sound I hear now
is the clock upon the wall . . .

A Pearce

GROWING UP

Do you remember that day
at Enniscrone?
You kicked off your sandals
And disappeared.
Into the silky dunes.

Your small silhouette paused
at the brim.
Scanning the horizon
For new opportunities.
I wiped my brow,
And you were gone.

On to the everlasting peace
of the sand.
On to the unknown
Atlantic waves.

Carole Buchanan-Brown

NIGHT TIME

Can the thoughts so truly work
With vibes, that really make us shirk
Our wish to stay here, on the right
And wait the onset of the night.
With all its kept usage
Moving on to its next stage
The dark time nudgings
Mingling with all other things,
That only erupt to life
When we poor mortals leave the strife
Of daily toil. The nights soft cooing
With total cosiness ensuing.
All beasties going forth to greet
Their friends with glee, and treat
Each separate group with ease,
Fulfilling precise wish to please.
Enemies by species hostile ever
Seek to allay discourse but never
Do. The night time rambles excel
The dawn draws near and so farewell.

Richard Saunders

WAITING

I look out the window
You're not there
I check the time
You're not there
My heart begins to ache
How much more can I take
I love you, you don't love me
What you can get
You take for free
With no strings attached to me.

L Wood

FOXES AT EASTACOTT

Summer-sleeping on the lawn outside, I woke one day
with the sun just up to catch the aeroplane's twin shining trails above,
but still too low for figleaf shadows on my face,
and there, three feet away, was a half-grown cub.
We looked with curiosity, then with a natural silent grace
he turned to the fig tree's darkness and walked unhurriedly away.

Another still early morning, sleeping out, sun higher up the sky,
with crows sitting, settling and rising on the wind-flattened corn,
the fox came trotting, quick (in its earlier sense) and brown
- is it too anthropomorphic to think perhaps it was glad to have been born?
and jumped, not over the typist's lazy dog, but up at the crows
scattering like burnt bonfire - paper, knowing he'd certainly miss,
sprang like a puppy racing among seagulls, dottily alive,
and I thought, delighted, 'Aesop must have slept out like this'.

Woken sometimes in winter by heart-stopping screams
I know that the vixen walks in the wood below;
but the dog-fox bark, sharp, interruptive, wakes my dog too,
A placid Labrador, warm in her cushioned kitchen box,
she barks, retalliative, at this harsh sound out of the dark.
As shouting downstairs won't stop her, we open the window wide
and shout and beam the torch to column out a long line of light
ending against the trees below. At last silence both in and out,
leaving us listening to the stillness of the night.

The fox walked, almost full-grown, by the bottom orchard hedge,
slim and most beautiful with chestnut-russet coat
black legs and tip to fur-round heavy tail,
inspecting and bruised and muddied windfalls on the ground,
taking a random bite or rolling one over with neat foot.
Then finding one to his taste - green Bramley looking too large a size
for his slim pointed muzzle - he trotted off proud of his new-found prize.

Pamela Gott

I AM NEVER ALONE

I feel a presence I cannot see
There is always someone just behind me
It always stands to my right,
But not near enough for me to sight

I've tried to catch it unaware
But there's nothing there for me to stare
It's a presence of love I feel
Don't ever leave me you are so real

Maybe it's the presence of one I loved and lost
Who's here to help me count the cost
They help me when I'm feeling low
Dear presence please don't ever go

I feel no fear about this cause
But fear has been my constant source
Fear that one day I shall lose
One I hold dear but could never choose

Maybe when my time arrives
That presence will be by my side
Then move to ones that I love so
And wrap them in their loving glow

Patricia Stamp

FOR HAYLEY'S BAPTISM
(Can be sung to the tune of 'Morning has Broken')

Jesus shine on her; shine all about her
Washing her freely; washing her white.
Gently redeem her, remove her transgressions
So she can now be pure in your sight.

Jesus shine on her, that others may see you
Reflected in her eyes and know of your love
Speak from her mouth Lord, and touch from her fingers
Make her feet willing to fly as your dove.

Jesus shine on us; fill us with your power
Making us soldiers to fight the good fight
Give us the courage: give us the wisdom
Extending your kingdom, the kingdom of light.

Yours is the power, yours is the glory,
Yours is the honour (Just see what he's done!)
Sing praise to the Father and praise to the Spirit
And glorify Jesus, God's wonderful son.

Heather Bushnell

BETTER DAYS

Blow me to the wind
Till I reach the light
Lifting gently to the blue
See my eyes forever honest
For Mother Earth
Dreams in a heart hoping for
that certain day
Good times lie waiting looking
to be found.
Though pieces of blue the
Darkness of loneliness
Guilded by the heavens
To better days
I long for better days
I live for better days

Andy Ryan

THE NIGHT

The clouds nestle over the hills protecting and caressing them as
the night slowly begins to move in.
The sun no longer visible except for a warm glow smudged onto the horizon.
The trees begin to take on forms, silhouetted standing proud almost fearless.
An artist's impression of blue, grey and black sweeps before us shrouding our view.
The moon now visible rising as the proud monarch of the sky,
Her suitors the stars amass in admiration.
The senses of the night begin to a wake once more, bristling with
anticipation aware of every touch sound and smell,
The night is now alive, so now will be my imagination vulnerable but
free to explore.
As I walk I become part of the night engulfed in a darkness my mind
releases, reaching out to feel and to soak in all that is around me.
Trees are now no longer, they become hands, some friendly, some my
enemies wanting to drag me still further into my imagination.
But as I look at the stars I know that they will guard and protect me
for I now belong with them as part of the night.

Susan Bill

SHADOWS

Shadows are black
They're dark and cold,
They seem to follow you wherever you go,
In the night they walk with you
Sometimes they seem to talk to you.

When you walk past a light
They seem to grow big with fright,
Then they shrink like someone you hate
When you're walking and it's late.

When you look round
they do to,
they seem to do what ever you do.

They lurk in your bedroom,
They lurk in your street
They hide in your bathroom,
But nobody knows,
Shadows.

Martin Makinen

BEAUTIFUL SOMERSET

Down in deepest Somerset,
Where cider apples grow,
We talk a funny dialect,
And our scarecrows - scare the crow.

Our meadows are of emerald green,
Cows give us creamy milk,
We have the best kept secret,
Our cheese tastes just like silk.

Farmers' wives bake our bread,
It really is quite grand,
And you should try our pickles,
They're always in demand.

Trout swim up our rivers,
And badgers scurry round,
In this beautiful Somerset county
Waiting to be found.

Pat Taylor

BONNY BLUEBELL

When I was young I had a doll,
I named her Bonny Bluebell,
She was my closest confidante,
To her my secrets I would tell.
She closed her eyes, and moved her limbs,
Just an ordinary doll was she,
But for most of my happy childhood years
Was like a precious babe to me.
And when from too much hugging
Her little arms fell off,
I sat down and made another pair
From a piece of pink cotton cloth.
I wheeled her out in a small doll's pram,
Had a cot for her as well,
For years I loved that little doll,
My pretty Bonny Bluebell.
Today's dolls walk and talk and sing,
Some drink and wet a nappy,
But do they make their little owners
Really quite as happy,
As I was with my Bluebell,
Who meant so much to me,
The doll I found one morning,
Beneath a Christmas tree.

Ivy Neville

FROM WITHIN

Virgin window waiting
for that ideal view.
In order to step beyond the window
I only think of you.

Virgin page of sonnets
trying to express emotion.
Ideally searching for
sense behind all of this commotion.

Virgin hearts of true romance
is scarce throughout the world
but in my world of make believe.
Romance is unfurled.

Virgin touch
upon my skin
releases absolute devotion
from within.

Natalie Turner

REMEMBERING

Bells of blue,
Buttercups of gold,
I will remember when I am old,
Running through meadows,
Climbing up trees,
Over the fences,
Scraping my knees,
Lying in haystacks
The drone of the bee,
Mother calling me in for tea,
Bread and butter, cakes and jam,
What a lucky girl I am.
Bells of blue,
Buttercups of gold,
These things I will remember
When I am old.

Val Davies

FRONT LINE

I feel like a hammered soldier
on the front line,
lying low in muddy trenches -
doing time.
I feel like a battered soldier,
with no food or sleep,
Paying tribute to my country -
Lying low - hiding deep.
My emotions are exhausted
my resources running thin,
My movements are very heavy
I wear a tortured grin,
my heart is very weary,
I can hardly speak or see,
overhead the sky is crackling,
shrapnel falls about me.
I feel like a hounded soldier
on the front line
A wounded tiger in hiding,
biding her time -
but when the wounds have healed,
and this war has been won,
I'll book myself a holiday,
In the faraway Florida sun.

Cheryl Poole

WHAT PRICE VICTORY?

Long dead the men who laughed, and once loved;
Who felt the warmth of summer sun;
Who took young wives and fathered children;
Whose happy lives had years to run:
Their country stole their love and laughter
And issued them with pack and gun.

Rows and rows of wooden crosses,
Earth mounds far as eye can see:
Was it worth the pain and suffering?
Was it hell! The victory
Is no reward to grieving mothers
Mourning sons who won't return:
Damn and curse the politicians!
May their souls forever burn
And rot in hell for this
Their pleasure; theirs the guilt;
They'll never learn.

Graham Manuell

THICK IN ACCENT ONLY

You've heard we're cider drinkers,
But that isn't always true.
You think that we're all *'varmer'* types,
That ploughing's all we do.

You've drawn a mental picture
Of the style of our attire,
Prolific use of baler twine
To keep our trousers higher.

Sou'wester hat upon thee head,
The smocking on the shirt,
The change of English diction,
Words like *'ooh'* and *'arr'* and *'gurt'*.

But if you think we're yokel types
You've got the wrong idea,
For Somerset's a clever place,
We're all quite wise down 'ere.

Leza Webb

REMEMBRANCE

(Written for the widow of my husband's closest friend who died January 1994, after 30 years of marriage)

I stand alone now - and remember,
The times we had,
The laughter and love - and friendship,
For good, for bad.
And then I wipe away a little tear,
And smile a small smile,
For I feel you still near - close by,
And all the while
Helping me to live out my time on earth,
Until the time of our rebirth.

Sometimes I feel guilt for things unsaid,
Undone and unremarked,
But I know within my heart, within my head,
For certain, for sure,
That you would not want me to feel this way,
Remorseful, regretful,
But instead be grateful for each single day,
We spent together,
And face the future with my head held high,
And the certain knowledge you're still nearby.

Janet R Booth

DOGMA (IS A BITCH)

Whoever asked the question
(And I think it's rather odd)
'Oh did we come from monkeys
or did we come from God?'

Now DNA is complex
And the universe is big
And the only fruit of the fig tree
Is normally the fig.

So if any of you feel clever
And dogmatic about the flood
Try rolling a daffodil flower
Back into its bud.

Jim Badman

TAVY TO TAMARA

I roared my love so loud, so fierce,
That, fearing my uncouth embrace,
Gentle Tamara fled from me.
At last, despairing, weeping, she fell,
Dissolved in tears.

Now bereft,
I watch the ripple of her lovely limbs,
The sparkle of her eyes, the waves of her hair
Flowing away from me for ever.
And I see her tears, her flooding tears.

I feel my own dull eyes grow damp,
My throat ache, till I throw myself
About the ground and howl my grief.
Now my limbs begin to loosen,
My body to lengthen and melt and stretch
Towards the sea.

With a shout
I am running down the hill, beside
My love, my beautiful Tamara,
My waves laughing and leaping for joy.
I shall be beside her now
While rivers flow.

J Wiltshire

AT THE AKBAR NIGHT-CLUB

The girls were up for sale,
No doubt about that.
The dance-floor was the shop window.
Men, no, shadows
Grouped about the edges.
The music lured them not
To dance.

They watched.
Flesh, just flesh
Bobbing, shaking,
Curving deliciously.
And fresh young faces,
Long, gleaming hair,
Delighting in their youthful excesses
The girls danced
And shook with little yelps of joy,
Sometimes oblivious to their purpose.

They recognised our need
Which was to dance
Sometimes we joined them
And they were glad
And applauded our moving rhythm
And the human feeling we brought
Which dispersed the shadows
For a while . . .

Edna Carmichael

MY FRIEND

My friend, I know you are hurting
You try just once in a while
Your eyes have lost their lustre
Your sighs belie your smile.

My friend how can I help you
What words will give you life
I try to give you comfort
But you cut me like a knife

My friend I step back slowly
Letting you know I care
When the time is right for talking
You know I will be always there.

My friend please know I love you
We shared so many times
The love out weighs the hurting
I'm here, till the clock of life chimes.

My friend of joy and sorrow
My friend of many happy years
I feel such fervent sorrow
I have shed so many tears

When the time is right for mending
The bridges will fall quickly into place
The shadow which has fell between us
Will disappear from your lovely face

Your path perhaps takes you onward
A life far away from me
But the friendship I feel lingers
Forever, friends we always will be.

June Woodward Martin

ROYAL VISIT!

At 4.15 the first cock-crow, so up and out of bed! We go the Royal
Cornwall Show. Why so early? Ask you may! It's June the 9th, 1989
a special day, thousands will be on their way:
Her gracious Majesty the Queen and Prince Phillip will be seen at
this show where they've not yet been.
Must make a clatter, wake the rest, an early start is always best,
let's put their good will to the test.
Near 7.00 as the showground lies flagwavingly before our eyes,
while clouds and sun rival the skies.
Until 11.00 all the crowd are ambling leisurely about to view
the showground's vast lay-out.
Authoratively, smart in black, Police are walking fore and back
to clear a good wide Royal track.
A waist-high crush-bar-screen unfolding along the walk-about is holding
effectively us *One And All* in. The Police cordoned magically,
quietly and with dignity to absolute efficiency.
An airobatic plane up high does antics in the cloudy sky, we stand
and wait, glad that it's dry. Nearly two hours such went by.
Cameramen now on the scene: 'Her Majesty our gracious Queen'
arrived, all dressed in emerald-green.
We see her smile, we are enchanted, the moment everyone has wanted
to come is here, Royally granted. The sky has also brightened up!
We take our fotos and we clap - we clap and snap and clap . . .
Then as the afternoon progressed, our gracious Queen gave to The Best
Cups and Awards and they felt blessed.
All over now, the Royal Pair is leaving to get back by air
to the Royal Home they share.
We quietly sing just within: '*God* save the Prince, *God* save the Queen!'

Marie Nanny Dowrick

NIGHT

Night falls! Behind the village church spire high
   The fiery sun sinks peacefully to rest,
While scudding cloudlets float across the sky
   Like weary angels resting on its breast.

A nightingale in lonely splendour sings
   To thrill the woodland with its melody,
And sheltering her chicks beneath her wings
   A blackbird settles in the apple tree.

Stand silently and listen - you may hear
   A drop of dew that settles on a rose,
A beetle scuttling 'neath a leaf in fear,
   The tiny petals of a daisy close.

A breeze that stirs the fluttering daffodils,
   The cluck of moorhen from her muddy bed;
A river, gliding gently through the hills
   The moon reflected in its silver thread.

The bark of vixen hunting for her young;
   The croak of bullfrog from a stream nearby;
While high above it all the stars are hung
   Like jewels in the velvet of the sky.

Night falls! A world of memory abounds
   And, listening, my sightless eyes can see
The beauty and the wonder in the sounds
   Of night, to whom night is eternity.

Freda L Norton

THE MORRIS DANCERS

The sound of music, somebody claps,
and here they come, those comely chaps.
Handkerchiefs are waving, smiles are broad,
these are the Morris Men, by everyone adored.
With a clunk and a click of a stout ash stick
and the merry jingle of bells.

With braces, ribbon and rosette,
hat at a rakish angle set,
knee breeches showing a shapely calf,
a wicked gesture to make you laugh.
With a clunk and a click and a stout ash stick
and the merry jingle of bells.

Weaving in the weaving out,
giving those staffs an almighty clout,
handkerchiefs twirling, slapping of thighs,
faces shining, sparkling eyes.
With a clunk and a click of a stout ash stick
and the merry jingle of bells.

Bodies are swaying and feet are tapping,
faces are smiling and hands are clapping:
A final flourish and it's over, and then
we'll drink a toast to the Morris Men.
With a clunk and a click of a stout ash stick
and the merry jingle of bells.

Brenda Heath

SUMMER IN THE FOREST

Beneath the canopy of trees
As I tread the path of the forest floor,
I hear the sigh of a gentle breeze
And feel at one with nature once more.

I lie among the flora and fauna
Within the shade of a giant oak
Sheltered from summer's steamy sauna
Wrapping solitude around me like a cloak.

The creatures of the wood ignore me,
Sensing that I mean no harm
Even the snake that slithers before me
Is part of my wooden temples' charm.

Upon the edge of a glistening pond
A spider weaves its web of lace,
And ferns unwind their leafy fronds
While butterflies flutter by with grace.

The sun sends down its golden rays
Through dappled leaves and branches high,
Oh, how I love these halcyon days
When all my worries from me fly.

When at last the sun sinks low
It's time to leave my leafy dome
In the beauty of the sunset's glow
Reluctantly, I head for home.

Freda Pilton

VOICES

I went to the wood one Autumn Day
Near where I lived as a child.
Where Village children gathered to play
And to witness life in wild.

They'd spend almost all their off school hours
Their voices with the birds would sing
They'd dance and play midst woodland flowers
'Twas a wonderful, glorious thing.

I'm sure the trees enjoyed the sound
Of those voices so happy and gay.
They seemed to stand and look around,
In their stately majestic way.

But now the wood is silent and grave,
Not a child to be seen or heard.
No chatter, no laughter, no sound, save
That of a solitary bird.

I watched as the leaves come tumbling down
As I stood in that woodland dell.
But it wasn't leaves that touched the ground
It was tears from the trees that fell.

The wind that passed through the baring trees
Was the sound of a million sighs
To remember the way things used to be
I quietly closed my eyes.

As I tried to recall those childhood days
The wood lived again it seemed
Had I heard those voices of children at play?
Or had I just hopefully dreamed?

Fear not great Ash, great Beech and Oak.
I don't think you need despair.
Can't you hear them as you stand in silent hope?
These voices! Yes they're still there.

Des Jones

NIGHT OUT

I'm going to the disco
My hair's set up in spikes.
I don't think it does much for me,
But it's what my boyfriend likes.

We gather, madly, chewing gum.
The girls glare at each other.
The bouncers close in all alert.
They think we stand for bother.

The night too soon draws to a close.
Punks and rockers reach the door.
What the bouncers thought might happen did.
Several bodies hit the floor.

All hell broke loose.
Out went the light
Glass scattered far and wide.
They thumped and whacked till out of breath.
They vanished into the night.

There came the roar of motorbikes
As friend and foe departed
With promises and shouted threats
To finish what they'd started.

B Bisgrove

REMEMBERING THE PAST, PRESENT AND FUTURE

Rows and rows of valiant men
Marching by
Heads held high
Tears in their eyes
Remembering the dead once again.

Rows and rows of mothers and wives
Waited in vain
Still feeling the pain
Their memories remain
Of their men who lost their lives.

Rows and rows of planes filled the air
Some had bombed towns
Some were shot down
Never found
Scattered who knows where.

Rows and rows of craft on the waves
Carriers and hospitals they have been
Battleship and submarine
Many more cannot be seen
Deep in watery graves.

Rows and rows of headstones white
In perfect formation
Naming someone's relation
Names from all nations
Who died to make everything right.

Rows and rows of us stand and look on.
Some with a gladness
Some with a sadness
Realising the madness
No war will be the last one.

Karen Cook

AT A PATCHWORK QUILT EXHIBITION

Conceived in the mind of Mary - A virgin,
Born on a scrubbed table, somewhere in America,
Slowly, painfully with sharp injections,
Tenderly, hands held me secure.
My life? Quiet mostly.
A colourful character some say.
Days and nights spent on my back,
weighed down by lovers old and young,
sullied by tears, blood and sweat.
Lay back, think of England!
Old now - I'm ready, wrapped for deportation.
No luxury cruise awaits.
Destination?
Bath, Somerset. The Old Country.
Foreign hands gently lift me,
No perfumed bedroom greets me,
A bare place
A cold place
A dim place
Away from joyous daylight.
They hang me!
My name at my feet,
'Rose of Sharon'
and *Please Do Not Touch*
Filing past curious eyes gaze up,
Kinfolk pay to see me.
A pale, tattered worn thing
Left to rot,
In vain I wait the Day of Resurrection.

B M Down

VENUS

Your face is the moon,
That glows in the night.
Your smile is the sun,
So warm and bright.
Your eyes are the stars,
Distant twinkling light.
Your hair an eagle,
That's free in flight.

Your lips are a rose,
Sweet blossom in spring.
Your hands are gentle,
Delicate butterfly wing.
Your voice sweetest music,
Only an angel could sing.
Your movement is poetry,
A very graceful thing.

Your heart's a diamond,
Of valve and desire.
Your present so warm,
A glowing winter's fire.
Your conversation so sharp,
No-one could tire.
You're a living Goddess,
That many admire.

Steve Bradshaw

LOW TIDE

Easy as men pull nets up the shore
or women curtains at dawn
the moon has pulled back
the powerless sea.

Traces remain:
finger-deep pools
and liquid twisting ribbons
left on a contoured vastness
of alien sand.

Fragments of sea,
stranded like its own creatures.
Merciless gulls will pick them clean
and the merciless sun burn up
the little wetness left by the moon.

The world stands upside down,
stone, slate, sky,
in the fleeting shallow wetness.

The sand dries white.
Reflections vanish.
Laughing naked children
run safe on the hot sand.

The sea is dispossessed
until the thin white moon
shall choose
to dictate
its next return.

Grace Ayling

DARTMOOR

Every day when I awake;
I go to the window and take;
My first good look of the day;
At the moors and fields;
That make me stay.

No town or city life for me;
No urbanised prosperity;
Just views to thrill;
Moor, wild and free;
And joy, that always comes to me.

Whether riding out;
Or walking alone;
On the moors I feel at home;
Although I take care to respect;
The awesome conditions it can project.

I'll never leave;
Or at least I hope;
Unless newcomers spoil our moat;
Of isolation that we love;
By changing it from above.

Kill the wild and make it tame;
Urbanise that's the game;
Safe little gardens;
Nice street lights;
Is this all to be our plight?

So please consider before you move;
Just what you may remove;
By making it all civilised;
And killing the last wilderness to survive.

M W Cann

WHEREIN LIES PEACE

I know a place wherein lies peace;
A secret place where land meets sea.
Sheer cliffs of white from rock strewn shore
Rise up from jewelled pools at their feet.
A diamond path across the sea
Stretches from horizon's haze,
Inviting me to dance with the sun.
The gentle waves caress the sand
That lines the tiny scalloped cove.
The grassy terraces are kissed
Gently with the morning sun.
The wheeling gulls soar rapturously;
Their raucous shrieks betray their greed.
In Spring a primrose bank's in shade,
Like butter spread o'er crimplene leaves;
And wood anemones are seen
In a blue sheened carpet by a willow.
Black green snake-necked cormorants fly,
Fish-filled for their nestlings' needs;
Skimming the sea towards the crags.
As heat haze rises with summer sun,
The charlock's mustard flowers open,
And light the cliffs with flames of gold.
The tiny stars of pimpernel
Trail, trampled under foot,
Whilst red valerian grows so boldly,
Clinging to the clefted cliffs
Where grey wagtails dip into caves.
As Autumn's faded glory comes,
The succulent blackberries are shrouded
With white wispy Catherine wheels
Of old man's beard dying slowly.
But still the gulls fly overhead;
And when the Winter comes, the Turkey oaks
And bay trees keep their green alone.

Janet Lang

FROME IN BLOOM

Bizzie Lizzies in wheelbarrows, begonias in pots, pixies and little red gnomes
For seventeen years this has been my home, where I live in a sheltered home
Joined Holy Trinity, made many friends, I'm 86 now and nearing my end
From a derelict patch a garden I've made, dug and raked and wielded a spade
There's a lovely stone wall covered with ivy, a background for Mallow and Buddleia, all thriving,
Cleared all the weeds, thistles and nettles, thrown out tin cans and rusty old kettles,
Planted daffodils, wallflowers, cowslips, primroses, poppies, cornflowers and stocks,
Forget-me-nots blue, Love in the Mist, Haste to the Wedding and Lover's Kiss
Honeysuckle, Fuschias, Michaelmas Daisies, Marigolds, Pansies and pretty Iris,
On hot summer days we sit in the shade, and friends admire the garden I've made,
I hope that one day, when I am gone, someone who loves gardens will come along
And weed it and tend it with loving care, and that it will flourish as if I'm still there,
We invite you to Frome a real Somerset town, it really is worth a visit
Cheap Street so quaint, Apple Ally, The Well, The Valentine Lamp on Catherine Hill,
The Round Tower, the river and beautiful churches
The people of Frome say, 'Home's where the heart is,'
When you go away, we hope you will say
We're so glad we didn't miss it.

Rose Anderton

DOCKYARD

Steel-grey hammer heads
stand to attention
while the siren echoes its Last Post
mournfully around them.

As one from all quarters
men and women spew forth from every exit.
Like blood from an opened vessel
draining life from a tired heart.
Cries of anguish, unheard.
Clutching hands, unseen, unheld.
A last breath of air
through brief-parted gates.

Sleek steel hull silently slipping
through rainbow-skinned waters.
Veteran voyager in peace and war,
returning to spill your sailors
overboard on endless leave.
Can you not yet stay to fight,
revive the vast womb-sheds
that spawned you?
In your turn giving life,
where now it falters and fails.

As you cast away and set sail
for sunnier climes and oceans,
new-found security and loyalties,
remember still your Mother land.

And the haggard, bitter faces
beneath the rusting hammer-heads
still standing
to no-one's attention.

Emily Wright

PROBLEMS DEFINED

As vanishing land dissolves from view
A sense of calm throughout the crew
As soft white crests, who gently creep
Caress the blue, so smooth, yet deep.
A shoal of silver, reflections glisten
Not a sound . . . I sigh, then listen
As silence breaks, a distant clap
The far off skies are turning black.
The stillness, now begins to rock
As fear strikes down upon my flock
'Batten down the hatches,' the violent wind whirls
With mighty breakers, the cruel sea swirls.
As lightning cracks a towering mast
A flash of horror for ships of past
The crashing post, I let out a cry
Convinced it is my time to die . . .

Awaking - as we idly sail
Tranquillity and peace prevail
As life itself, is true to form
A lull before, and after the storm!

Lyn Constantine

CORNISH GARDEN

Tamarisk and veronica
Are lovely when they grow
Together in the garden
Of a cottage near Portloe.

Beyond, the gorse sun-ripened
Lends fragrance to the air,
Flying her golden banners
From Jacka to Manare.

Carpet of thyme, bee-clustered
Is spread to the shore below,
Where thrift in each rocky crevice
Makes, sea-fringed, a garden grow.

Above on this rocky splendour,
Above on the cliff near Portloe,
In a magical sea-girt garden,
Veronica, tamarisk, grow.

Purple and proud veronica,
Tamarisk, feathery, fair,
While the gorse streams her golden pennons
From Dodman to distant Nare.

G E M Tamlin

NOVEMBER

The scent of burning leaves
drifts through the curling smoke
from smouldering bonfires
at the garden's edge;
new fruit is land in store,
chutney, and Marrow jam,
there's green tomatoes
on the window ledge;
Now in the early dark,
the street lamps seem to stand
like guardian angels,
draped in misty rain,
The sun hangs in a shrand,
the trees are silhouettes,
only the Robin sings -
November's here again!

Freda Pearson

DEAR HUSBAND

I'm writing this letter with your good in mind,
Tho' truth can be painful, it's meant to be kind.
I've been preparing your robes and it's quite plain to see
There's much more of you now than there used to be.
I've let out your waistband and seams quite a bit.
Put a double width gusset in the place where you sit.
You're a triple X now but I really do fear
A XXXX won't fit you by this time next year!
You came back the last time all bruised black and blue
Complaining the chimneys were too small for you.
The answer, dear husband, is a really strict diet,
And I beg that for your sake you really will try it.
Without it, I tell you, the reindeer will strike -
And Rudolph suggests that you 'get on your bike!'
With your weight on board they will never get lift off
So they'll either dump you - or leave every gift off.
Just think of the grief that will cause girls and boys
Who leave you mince pies in exchange for their toys.
And there lies the problem, though each leaves you but one,
By the end of the night you have eaten a ton.
And the drink that you sink as you go on your way
Could find you in trouble . . . 'drunk driving' your sleigh!
I *must* write to all children, leave no goodies this year
Or you might go off *Pop* and just disappear!
                Your loving, worried wife,
                    Mrs Claus.

Doreen J Jones

TO MAIA

The beginning.
Not for us.
Our beginning has passed unnoticed
By any but us.

Your wakeful churning greets the day as if,
By chance,
You knew that sunlight
Streamed
Beyond your fluid world,
Beyond the world of shadows and muffled sounds,
To hearts that welcome your presence,
Your fire,
Your life.
The life that is your own.

Your protector waits with baited breath:
Eyes open,
Gaze fixed on the unknown.
How will our meeting be heralded?
Let us be open to truth.

Soon we will meet.
You begin the shortest
And the longest
Journey of your life.

Use it well.

Find your own space.

Make your mark.

Mark your place in humanity.

Ros Ashton Butler

DEJA-VU

I know this place like migrating birds.
I've even heard those exact same words.
Yet everything and every sound.
Is coming at me on the rebound.
Colours and smells are unfamiliar
The whole idea is getting sillier.
Have I really been here before.
How many times have I seen that door.
Do I really know this place.
It should be as familiar as my face.
Memories are stirred, an unrippled surface
I should remember it like my first kiss.
Bright flashbacks ignite a memory
Of a place that feels old to me.
It's scary when a moment, a time and place.
Feel familiar and yet so out of place.
This place I don't know so well as I thought.
Is it somewhere deep down that I've sought.
A deep rootedness of an inherent past
What a pity this feeling won't last.

Nick Stevens

EXMOOR

Stone, stone, stone, stone, stone, stone, stop.
Quick step, bold leap, startled hop.
Down grass, down grass, mud, mud; stuck.
Pull hoof, pull hoof, mud, mud, suck.
Out and run, out and run, crippled soggy hoof.
Stamp and test, test and stamp. Crippled soggy hoof.
Away, away, down scree-filled dip.
Stop; shelter in scree-filled dip.

Sky, sky, and pain-filled cry.
Black of night and blue of sky.
Spray of stars and shapes of sheep,
White, white shapes on slopes, so steep.
But Soggy Hoof - no more, no more,
But more and more of heathy moor.
And so to lie in sinking mire,
To lie, to lie in death's own fire,
The rotting carcass of my sheep
rots alone, rots fast, and oh, so deep.
Blood and blood, bone on bone
is buried deep in stone on stone.

Hannah Pratt

SEA-SIDE TRAIN - ST IVES 1930'S

The train whistle blew loud and clear on every hour for all to hear,
We all look up to the bridge on the hill
to see the white smoke as it stands there still.
Everyone looks, it's a main event, eager faces from every tent
peer up from their selected sand, to see the sight they know is grand.
Children rush to open spaces anxious looks upon their faces.
Will he? Won't he? Once again wave down to them from on his train.
The train comes on now past the gap, all the children start to clap.
The engine and the children sigh as it slows upon the bridge up high.
All eager with anticipation as it pulls into the station.
He is there now, he's so brave. The engine driver gives a wave.
Hurrah! All is safe to dig and play. The engine driver waved again today.

Humphrey Noall

INJUSTICE

Naturally a philanthropist
But now solitary,
Desperately alone
With no sweet thoughts for companionship.

Only the distant reminiscence
Of a vague contentment,
Easily defeated
By savage and untameable spirit.

Desolation and dislocation,
Mournful melancholy,
Damned despair storm
Wildly, smashing a former peace.

Thoughts swarm for the minds attention, like
A plague of mosquitos
Viciously biting flesh
To conquer their bloodthirsty craving.

Tranquillity not now existing
No mere trace to be found.
Mental chaos rules - hard,
With totalitarian power.

Anger, misery, torment, torture.
Immense loneliness.
Why can solace not declare its arrival?
What beast provokes such anguish and pain?

The injustice of unrequited love.

Lisa Vanstone

DROUGHT'S END

The darkness comes and with it comes the rain,
Evening's black clouds send raindrops beating on the pane,
Yet I lay dry and snug beneath the covers,
Seeking sleep and rest for tired eyes and brain.

Drowsily I picture soil devouring welcome rain,
Each tiny thread of root below,
Will stretch out to suck up God's lifeline,
Knowing with His sun and rain is the only way to grow.

I'm happy that the rain has come at last
To cover naked river beds and lakes
The pitter patter neither annoys nor worries me,
I truly hope it rains till morning light awakes!

Then what a difference I shall see,
Parched grass tipped green simply overnight,
Leaves and plants perkily pointing skywards,
Once again, God has seen His world alright.

Why do we ever doubt His answer
To prayers, hesitantly, yet hopefully, said,
Patience is never a strong point with us mortals,
Yet the Provider knows our needs, though often left unsaid.

Long ago He sent a rainbow after floods,
His promise to Noah then, still holds us in good stead,
'There will be a time for planting and a time for harvest'
Secure in that promise, I snuggle further in my bed!

P Heppel

MISSING PIECES

Rain on the window
And tears on my cheek
My strength is inside
The comfort I seek

The pavements are icy
A storm brews outside
I'm safe by the fire
Whilst from you I hide

My thoughts are electric
My face gives no clue
Of the pain and the tears
That I've cried over you

Flames crackle with life
They're dancing for me
Their fiery tongues
Seem bright and carefree

I'm lost in the flames
Transfixed by the sight
They crackle in contrast
With the black cloak of night

These nights by the fire
Warm me within
Rebuilding and watching
My new life begin

Darkness surrounds me
Embraces me tight
A blanket of sleep
Creeps out of the night

Dawn Coull

GENEALOGY

He seeks me here
he seeks me there
is there nowhere left to hide
an empty room
or little hole
that I can crawl inside

Documents, Bonds
and age old Wills
are always in my hand
and only another
nut like me
could ever understand

My obsession I know
is wearing thin
and I do try to keep in control
but my eyes alight
at the wondrous sight
of a Register, Hearth Tax or Poll

My husband just hates
those baptismal dates
though with pride I do delve in the past
but I've run out of places
and odd little spaces
he keeps finding them all much too fast

So give me a phone
if like me you're alone
because life, past and present, gets tough
and I'll do what I can
while I'm dodging my man
to help you, and pray it's enough.

Lesley Bull

RIVER SONG

Rising gently in the highlands
Full of life, clean and gay
Bubbling joyfully down the mountains,
The river's singing, on its way.

In the hills, gaily rushing,
Over tors and heather cliffs.
Free to dance, clear and shining
Homo Sapiens are a myth

Softly coiling through the valleys
Gripping boulders, cold and grey
Pushing stagnant weeds asunder,
Sliding greenly into modern day.

Through the towns, gliding unnoticed,
Busy mums, ignore its flow.
But little Johnny is in danger,
With plastic boats - nowhere to go.

Past the factory walls it judders.
Oily now, its ripples closed.
Towering chimneys, smoke embellished.
Reflect the misery, enhance the cold.

Striving now, to clear its image,
It ventures through the rural clime.
Collecting agricultural slurry,
Plus residues of slag and lime.

Filthy, oily, full of grime.
It can't retreat, there's but one way,
Towards the sea, to end it's life
The river's sung - its life away.

Heather Beer

RETURNING TO DARTMOOR

The stillness around me has lifted
away all coverings to my inner being.
I feel vulnerable now -
My soul is whispering towards
the vision my eyes see.
I try to turn away -
to reach beyond this feeling,
But gently -
So sweetly - I am embraced,
Silently,
My spirit cries
for the reality which lies
Just in front of me.

Jane Ifold

MY SILVER SHADOW

Golden orbs of light
seek me out in the darkness
The thoughts are mine
But the visions are the night's possession.
Gone are the days of lost worlds?
Will I wonder no more
Neath the golden rays of the autumn sun?
Will my ways always be dark
Or will my enlightenment come.
I reach out for you my Silver Shadow
With both arms I gladly embrace thee.
But you dwell beyond my periphery
And only in the night visions
You reveal yourself
How long must I search?
For your doorway...

K G Gray

CAVERNS AND CAVES

Mysterious, eerie, dark and damp,
Hiding so much if you're without a lamp.
Dripping and echoing for those who are brave,
Courageous enough to explore a cave.

Stories untold have happened down here,
Smugglers have stored their caskets of beer.
Tunnels so long, twisting around,
If you lose your way, you'll never be found.

Hanging so long, standing so tall,
Stalagmites, stalactites guard a wall
Glistening like diamonds, sparkling like gems,
Tunnels get darker with all the bends.

Tread very carefully, step with great stealth,
Will a great find increase your wealth?
There's danger around with bats
flying high,
Squawking their warnings of ghosts
floating by.

Caverns are there if you have the
right mind,
Hidden so deeply, their openings to find.
With a true kind of courage and a
lack of great fear,
There's treasure awaiting for those
venturing here.

Elizabeth Holland

SEEING THROUGH

My brother, when we meet, I'd rather you could see
not the elephant indignant in a thundery sky,
nor the chiselled cliff-edge stag, nobly challenging why,
nor the heavy-headed gander all too ready to defy;
but the open-arm glow of the applewood fire,
and a sharing pot of tea. . .
the Christ Spirit within me!

My sister, when we meet, I'd smile if you could see,
not the copulating cockerel conspicuous and loud,
nor the dog-eared dance of mating that hugs you like a shroud,
nor coachboy charm that turns to pumpkins when it's left the cooing crowd;
but the dry-your-boots glow of the peat-log fire
and a mug of honesty. . .
the Christ Spirit alert within me!

My neighbour, when we meet, I'd be cheered if you could see
not monotonous horizons that drizzle from nine to five,
nor the shoulder stoop and eyelid droop from the weight of being alive,
nor another body on the pension path intending to survive;
but the let-it-be glow of the starlit fire,
and toasted cheese with your tea. . .
the Christ Spirit awake within me!

My lover, when we meet, I'd relax if you could see
not the little lamb with the help-me bleat dancing with his doubt,
nor the rag-doll rascal who's lost his thread and hopes you'll sort him out,
nor the compendium of party games that spins the curfew out;
but the safe-at-home glow of the heartfelt fire
and the shiver of moon in the tea. . .
the Christ Spirit aroused within me!

Dauda Zai

THE FORMER YUGOSLAVIA

As the nights get darker I watch with an aloof air,
The final gasps of this bright summer.
As the misinformation piles up on the TV screen,
Between the artistic salesmen and those design school trendies,
A new wave of flashy advertisements by tomorrow's
film makers - the budding Tony Scotts.
I turn to the sunset silhouetting the pointed church,
Sighing with horror as dead bodies litter Europe's streets
- all over again.
Gangsters who brutalise all that would inspire.
No solution - no cure for cancer
No Shangri-La with the lost secrets
Tibetan masters dead and tortured.
Our intellectual leaders seem self-centred
Ambitious Machievellians,
With the will to write based on career.
So they sit back (like your humble narrator)
Commenting on society like it's some dull pastime,
Lost in a world of impotent importance
Getting older, voting Tory,
Same old fucking story.

Paul Hilton

SPORTY HUSBAND, LAZY WIFE

My husband and I are as different as can be
He likes to go running and I don't agree;
He likes to go cycling five miles or more,
I find this kind of exercise a bit of a bore.

I run around the block with him,
For five minutes or more;
I keep telling myself it's good for me,
As I fall to the floor.

I try to support him,
I can honestly say;
It just isn't for me,
At the end of the day.

Beverly Woollacott

SPRING

The quiet and the peace in our fields of green,
Is broken only by the sound of sheep and cows.
    Spring time comes once more
And leaf and blossom to the bows.

Young rabbits hop out into this world, unknown
Are the dangers and horrors which could await.
    Spring time comes once more
And fox looks under the rough five bar gate.

The shimmering grass ripples to and fro,
It moves as waves when the wind passes by.
    Spring time comes once more
And the sun shines down from the cloudless sky.

The buzzard soars ever higher and higher,
Eyes look down for the prey which it seeks.
    Spring time comes once more
And suddenly a young rabbit shrieks and shrieks.

The quiet and the peace return to our fields of green.
The birds build their nests, which they try to hide.
    Spring time comes once more
And wild flowers bloom in our glorious countryside.

Gwendoline Jacobs

LIGHT

The light relates to your face
In almost splendid reflecting hope
Where the dark set eyes lie,
Waiting for an event
But not gratified by the moment.
The smooth, soft, white encapsulation
Holds the thoughts within the mind to die for.
The long black fibres atop
Complement the hue of eye
And tone of lip.
The moonlight is what I want
To see capturing this ensemble
In its beam;
Delaying speech till such a time when
Two towers stand alone,
Yet connected palpably
And by soul.
As this light dies
To be replaced by yet greater,
Profiles give the perfect outlook
But not showing
The real light beneath,
The light which shines on all
Who hear it -
The voice of the mind to die for
And the dark set eyes, the window -
Medium for this beam.

Martyn Ingham

A SACK OF JEWELS

I poached salmon,
Through December on their four week run.
Fierceness suddenly gripped me,
Then brutality.

In the secret of night,
I froze the prey in the powerful beam
Of a huge chrome lamp.
Thrusting an innocent garden fork,
Pinning a giant fish into the gravel below.

Flinging a huge thrashing curve
Of glazed silver into the stunned wood.
Wrapping him tight in a hessian shroud.
Staring eye and questioning mouth,
A sack of jewels, gasping.

Can the river forgive me?
For she would gush and spangle
Through her year.
Until my mind became entranced
Drawn by magnificent, awesome power.

Mighty fish come home,
In from the wild Atlantic,
To find their nursery pools.
The river proud and splendid.

Fish and water glittered as one,
In their winter celebration.
I watched, entranced
Gasping.

Keith Cozens

YOU!

Tears flowing freely,
Empty feeling,
Brown eyes closed forever,
The laughter lines,
The smile that once lit up your face,
Gone to another place,
Bitterness and sadness,
Hard to differentiate,
At one with each other,
Sitting alone,
Once a heart beat to hear,
Now silent forever,
The light that was you extinguished.

D L Redman

SWEET SEPTEMBER

Slightly chilly mornings; cool and balmy eves;
A touch of gold and crimson to early falling leaves.

Mellow rays of sunshine; lengthening twilight hours;
The freshness of a cooling breeze 'twixt light and heavy showers.

Skies of blue and silver; sea of sparkling glass;
Heather covered moorlands; beauty unsurpassed.

Misty far horizons; moonlit starry nights;
Butterfly migration; moths 'round candlelight.

Chrysanthemums and dahlias bathed in morning dew;
The heavenly scent of roses; honeysuckle too!

Blackberries and apples; gold and purple plums;
Preserving and conserving before the winter comes.

Thanksgiving for the harvest almost gathered in;
Children going back to school; autumn term begins.

The lingering kiss of summer; a hint of spring, long past;
The gentle smile of autumn 'ere winter's dye is cast.

This is sweet September, month of purest gold;
A time to be remembered as the year grows old.

Joan Wakeling

COUNTRY BLISS

When the four walls that surround me
Become more than I can bear,
I step beyond the threshold
Into the country air.
As I walk along the footpath
Beneath the swaying trees,
I feel the need to savour
Precious moments such as these.

Across the fields my journey
Brings me on to Wembury Bay,
The deep blue sea of summer
Now a chilly greenish grey.
The beach once filled with tourists,
Ice-cream, children, wasps and bees,
Is now clad with mounds of seaweed
Tossed up by stormy seas.

So now it's nature's chance again
To rule the rocky shore
And enjoy deserted silence
Now that winter's here once more.
Relaxed, refreshed and cold wind
Sharply cutting through my clothes,
I have the feeling great wealth
Only a country lover knows.

Lynne Betts

WITHYPOOL HILL

There was something about Withypool Hill -
A sense of time, that haunts me still,
Felt in the place where the ancient stones lie
And in the sadness of a buzzard's cry

As we walked on at a hearty rate,
Your footsure march, my stumbling gait,
You often waited, turned and smiled
As I once did when you were a child

And that was so short a time compared
To when they lived and how they fared -
The people who leave their traces still
And worshipped high on Withypool Hill

In a silver coloured monorail
With wistful stares and looking pale,
Sit the children of another age,
Who peer out from their germ-free cage

And learn about what life was like
When people could still run or hike
In moorland places where the air was free
And forgotten flowers were left to be

Maybe the magic will still be there
To help them find that something rare
When the past, present and future stand still
As they glide past a place called Withypool Hill.

Sandra Kershaw

INFORMATION

We hope you have enjoyed reading this book - and that you will continue to enjoy it in the coming years.

If you like reading and writing poetry drop us a line, or give us a call, and we'll send you a free information pack.

Write to

> Poetry Now Information
> 1-2 Wainman Road
> Woodston
> Peterborough
> PE2 7BU